# Acting, Learning, and Change

# Acting, Learning, and Change:
## Creating Original Plays with Adolescents

**JAN MANDELL
AND JENNIFER LYNN WOLF**

**Foreword by Shirley Brice Heath**

**HEINEMANN**
Portsmouth, NH

Heinemann
A division of Reed Elsevier Inc.
361 Hanover Street
Portsmouth, NH 03801-3912
www.heinemann.com

*Offices and agents throughout the world*

Cataloging-in-Publication data on file at the Library of Congress.

ISBN: 0-325-00321-1

Editor: Lisa A. Barnett
Illustrations: Katie Gass Gonzalez
Cover Design: Julie O. Vinette
Manufacturing: Steve Bernier

Printed in the United States of America on acid-free paper

07 06 05 04 03  DA  1 2 3 4 5

To my son
Jesse Lee Mandell McClinton
*JM*

In memory of my grandmother
Caroline Boquet Massen
*JLW*

# Contents

# Acknowledgments

We have looked forward to the time when we could sit down and thank the many people who have helped us bring this book to life. First and foremost, we wish to thank our students. Their courage and their stories are both the inspiration for and the evaluation of our work. We hope that those we have interviewed and written about will enjoy recognizing their voices (even when we could not identify all of them by name), since we have enjoyed thinking about them each time we sat down to work on these stories of their work with us.

We are indebted to the many organizations that not only saw promise in our work but also helped to fund it. The Spencer Foundation, long interested in the broadest possible definitions of education, has been generous in supporting our work. The General Electric Fund also contributed support, particularly through the enthusiasm and interest of Jane Polin, who believes as strongly as we do in the power of the arts in learning. The Carnegie Foundation for the Advancement of Teaching, under the guidance of Lee Shulman, also contributed to the project and encouraged us to see our teaching as scholarship along with our research into our students' ways of becoming instructors, mentors, and models. The National Research Center on the Gifted and Talented has supported our efforts to explore the promise of the arts in education. And while we wish to thank these organizations for their generous support, we in no way wish to imply that they are responsible for the opinions expressed in this volume; for that we take sole responsibility.

The St. Paul Companies Leadership Initiative in Neighborhoods Grant paid for travel and research into creative performing arts companies across North America. In addition, our school districts—the St. Paul Public Schools, the University of Minnesota Youth Studies and Social Work Departments, and the Cotati–Rohnert Park Unified School District—provided much-appreciated support with sabbatical leave, substitute time, teaching appointments, and administrators who showed a genuine interest in our work: Principal Mary Macabee, Principal R. Ken Clark, Principal Jan Gonzales, Superintendent Curman Gaines, and Superintendents Walter Buster and Jan Heffron.

Two St. Paul establishments have allowed us, over a period of four years, to work long hours on their premises for the price of a cup or two of coffee: Dunn Brothers Coffee and Caffé Con Amore. In addition, the Hungry Mind Bookstore in St. Paul (now The Ruminator) proved an invaluable resource by carrying an extensive selection of drama and education titles, and ordering more whenever we asked.

We are fully aware that we cannot claim sole authorship of the exercises presented in this book. Like all good theatre methods, they have evolved over time and have been shared among any and all performance artists working with young people. Listed here are those who have shared with and influenced us: Augosto Boal, Steve Dimenna, Free Street Theater in Chicago, Kay Hamlin, Brent Hasty, Ezra Knight, Gavin Lawrence, Marion McClinton, Laurie Meadoff and the CityKids Foundation, Jennifer Nelson, Doug Patterson and the Theater of the Oppressed in Omaha, T. Mychael Rambo, Rebecca Rice, Viola Spolin, John Stout, Tanya White, and James Williams, as well as Robert Alexander and the Living Stage Theater Company.

The essentials of a project like this are child care, word processing, research, red tape management, and all other manner of support. The following people offered deeply appreciated assistance with these tasks: Lacy Austin, Mary Burnison, Laurel Fardella, Darlene Fry, VeShon Tipler-Greenfield and Michael Greenfield, Tom Homme, Maggie Kessel, Elaine Kirshbaum, Kwame McDonald, Jan's sister, Susan Schwarz, Christy Smith, Jamie Sandhana Thompson, Dudley Voigt, and Marguarette Winston-Glover. And thank you to Karing Khalsa and Mere Piare and the quiet space they provided at their farm.

We are deeply grateful to the people who have taken time away from their own busy lives and projects to read and respond to our work: Arnetha Ball, Colleen Calahan, Sandra Massen, Paul Messaris, Rebecca Rice, Lissa Soep, and Shelby Wolf. Their thoughtful critiques strengthened our ideas. We also gratefully extend thanks to illustrator Katie Gass Gonzalez, whose figures bring our words to life while illustrating the importance of art in learning.

## Jan's Thank Yous

To the circle of people who share my passions, and believe in me unconditionally: Colleen Calahan, Dorothy Hoffman, Tom Homme, Meri Golden, T. Mychael Rambo, Mary Tinucci, James Williams, Kim Colbert, Luana, and Marion McClinton.

Finally, to my son, Jesse, who at all times reminds me of what is most important—our children and their futures.

## Jennifer's Thank Yous

To my family, always my most enthusiastic audience: Sandra and Charles Massen, Armand Massen, Reneé and Hal Peters, the Stalpers, the Stevens, and the Wolves.

To Shirley, for the invitation into this new way with words.

And to Rob, for listening to the stories.

# Foreword

*Shirley Brice Heath*
*Stanford University*

In an age when a general despair hangs about us over the diminishing importance of books, every foreword takes on a special urgency to plead for the decision to read this book before all others. This foreword is no exception, though the reasons for the plea in the case of *Drama, Learning, and Change* may be unique and entirely unexpected. This is a book that in a quiet, firm way gives startling twists and turns to several key ideas that have gained increasing strength over the past two decades in school reform and learning theory. This book upsets several generally held givens about teacher research as well as prevalent notions about how learning in school links with community knowledge, youth culture, and contemporary needs and concerns.

It is highly significant that the work here received bits and pieces of support from several funding groups not generally associated with one another. The Spencer Foundation, the General Electric Fund, and the National Research Center on the Gifted and Talented all played some part in either contributing to Wolf's travel to Minnesota to observe and participate in Mandell's classroom or in sponsoring research that inspired Mandell and Wolf to dig deeper, listen better, and question more intensely. Particularly important in this work has been the goal of the National Research Center on the Gifted and Talented to help teachers find new ways of thinking about the gifts and talents of their students as learners and explicators of their own cumulative skill and knowledge base. The Center has also been a stimulus for Mandell and Wolf to consider the importance of continuity and development for students across the years of their secondary schooling, not just within a few classes or specialized opportunities for the gifted and talented here and there. As will be evident in this volume, the students who speak out here in many roles represent a range of classes in acting and drama from the initial semester through several years of classes and community performances. An additional stimulus has been the work of the Carnegie Foundation for the Advancement of Teaching on teacher research and community learning. Their scholars have explored in numerous ways how the expectation of becoming a professional—whether as future teacher, actor, or public servant—enables the learner to take up the requisite specialized vocabulary, sense of self, and openness to learning from and about others.

Teacher research has within the past two decades experienced exponential growth, primarily as a component of school reform and professional development. Universities have increasingly been challenged to demonstrate their contributions to community and especially to improvement of teaching, test scores, and student engagement in public schools. Teacher education programs have rapidly turned to types of qualitative research, particularly case studies, to document what happens in classrooms and the social nature of student learning. Both of these pressures have led higher education professionals to link with teachers at the K–12 levels to study not only student learning, but also teacher change and conditions of professional development. Publications from these cooperative arrangements have come out by the dozens every month in journals and books, authored singly by university faculty as well as collaboratively by teacher and professor/teacher educator.

Another development has been the self-historicizing undertaken by individual teachers who have written narrative accounts of their teaching. A surprising number of such histories have come from individuals upon their exit from the profession. The local knowledge within these accounts has rarely conveyed the kind of powerful ideas about the practice of teaching that translate into general knowledge. Indeed, the quasi-sensational nature of some of these works has drawn a general readership who may well remember from such accounts primarily the difficult lot of students and schools today and little about the life and learning of teachers. Many such accounts are classroom-bound and do not follow teachers into the many other arenas of their work.

*Drama, Learning, and Change* steps away from all previous types of accounts of teaching by teachers or by teachers partnered with university researchers. This volume centers on teachers learning with one another and with students. Most of the action takes place in Mandell's drama classes in Central High School in St. Paul, Minnesota, where Wolf was often able to travel for observation and participation. Mandell, as the mother of a young child, could not travel to Wolf's English classroom in California with any frequency, but the two of them found ways to spend days together talking about the data, ideas of learning, and strategies for testing new ideas and explaining old ones.

Wolf, a drama and English teacher at the secondary level, learns with and through Mandell and her students in the classroom, and through the extension of their learning into community theater and careers beyond school. Central here is the question not of how Mandell and Wolf teach, but how they gain from taking a professional stance toward how and what their students learn. Their discussions unmask pedagogical practices that originate on some occasions from the teacher, but much more frequently from student interactions with textual material, performance and production standards, and return classroom visits from Mandell's former students, who now have careers in the arts world.

Mandell and Wolf did not begin their learning together under any illusion that they shared philosophies of teaching or of "doing drama" in the classroom; in fact, they knew they did not. However, what brought them together were their common concerns, queries, and qualms, as well as areas of confidence and conviction. The two teachers differ considerably in their ways of teaching, views of students, and modes of learning. Thus it would have made no sense for the teaching style of either to be the sole object of their joint study; instead they chose to focus on how the ongoing accumulation, correction, and retrying of knowledge occurred as students and teachers acted together in their learning.

What these two teachers manage to achieve is the difficult act of imagining one another in as much weight and solidity as possible through mutual study. The fact that some of their thinking about teaching is not the same—in some cases it's even contradicting—does not prevent their committing themselves to learning rather than to choosing among pedagogical practices. This book is testimony to the fact that any teacher has to move beyond technique, strategy, and fixed persona. Every year, every different group of students should supplement, complement, and contradict teachers' former convictions as well as their skills and knowledge.

Community knowledge, or the transferal, performance, and production of one's classroom learning into the community of one's daily life, sits at the heart of the approach of each of these teachers to learning. As together they watch students imagine and act out others within the drama classroom, they also hear students struggle to place themselves in the mental space of "otherness," "difference," and shifts of self identity. Taking risks together, as is the norm in drama workshops, is only the beginning. These students—and Wolf and Mandell—take on learning how to see and feel the world as another. In some cases, as with a hearing-impaired student in their class, this means learning to sign in order to communicate as another. In doing so, they accept the need to decouple their previous expectations of others and of themselves and thereby allow themselves to act out and feel within the changes brought by the role of another.

Extensive learning about the historical realities of race relations, gender inequities, neighborhood stereotypes, and discriminatory civic and police practices had to take place in order to make their practices and performances live. Students show throughout this volume not only what is like to take on the identity of another in robust fashion, but also what it is like to see and hear others reduce the "other" by painful subtraction or ignorance. Students explore how their racial and other physical or linguistic features may appear fearsome, loathsome, or so diminished as to be unworthy of notice. Together students study, both in history and in their own experiences, the plights of young people as segmented from both childhood and adulthood. Their roles examine their current state: general public dismissal as anything other than consumers, potential troublemakers, and inspiration for popular culture.

Both Wolf and Mandell learn from their students the importance of understanding that abilities consist largely in knowing not only how to do something, but also how to extend this doing in three essential ways. The first of these is to consider that when change comes very rapidly in context and contingencies, one's *doing* has to be calibrated by an ongoing sense of *what's right*. Thus no skill or bit of information acquired is in itself sufficient; one must also know when and how either technical skill or critical information must be altered under different circumstances. Nothing teaches this principle so well as theatre, when a missed cue or prop, unexpected audience reaction, or dropped line imposes immediate *redoing* on the part of other players.

A second and strongly linked essential is *interdependence in learning*. In theatre it is not enough for each person to learn as an individual; everyone's learning must be interdependent with everyone else's. Thus the group moves together, with individuals taking responsibility for a third essential that Mandell and Wolf explore jointly. Learning to do also means knowing how to demonstrate, explicate, or illustrate for others. Often within Mandell's classroom, the vision of a performance, as well as its depth and elaboration, comes as students work with one another, particularly as more advanced students from classes of previous years return to work with current learners. Students in this volume illustrate that they are equipped as practitioners who can not only do, but also articulate why they do what they do. The power of being able to address ethics, techniques, mistakes, successes, and challenges of learning through drama comes through to Mandell's students in every return visit from students of past years.

Perhaps most meaningfully, these students have opportunities through both Mandell and Wolf to perform and demonstrate their learning within their communities. Mandell has a long history of working with students in public performances for conferences, community theatre, and special events. Her classes and the work of her students carry respect, expectation, and responsibility throughout the region, as well as very powerfully within the locally active Penumbra Theater. Many articles and news releases extol the work of her students and their impressive, consistent record for high-quality performances. Wolf's students in arts and English classes have achieved a considerable reputation in her region. Through representation in documentary film and local performances, they have had opportunities to think about how they spend their time and how they explain choices they have made for their learning through art.

H. L. Mencken once said that those people Americans admire most are the most daring liars; those they detest are those who tell the truth. These teachers and many others who learn with their students through the dramatic act are those who make changes for the sake of truths, not only truths they can live with but also that they can help others come to consider. "Daring liars" is one way of looking at the standardized tests that many embrace as central to public school reform and to an increase in student achievement. Of course, in and of themselves, these tests have no will or intent, and those who endorse them generally know tests lie about the kinds of learning that matter most in medical, technical, and civic life. Recognizing that implausible ideas are often the very ones most worth exploring, seeing alternatives that may emerge with shifts of conditions, and knowing process beyond fixed facts and figures—these are the qualities without which modern science could not function. But an undeniable truth is that we see these as somehow too important, too vital, too essential for learning in school. Mandell and Wolf, acknowledging this point, lead all of us—students and teachers alike—to see the importance of enabling both classroom and community to be learning laboratories.

Trying not only to tell the truth but also to explore undeniable truths should be the lasting effect of this volume. Deniable truths are those truisms or myths that many of us hold onto with great force; these are the lies to which Mencken referred. With Mandell and Wolf, students begin to learn many painful, undeniable truths. Mandell and

Wolf make certain their learning environments feel the vigorous presence of competing ideas, of the uncertainties that lie beyond binary oppositions, and of the uneasy juxtapositions of expert and lay ideas. Finally, and most important, their actions and their words urge us to be responsible as *learning teachers* to one another.

# Introduction

> Art is the mirror, the only one in which we can see our
> true collective face. We must honor its sacred function.
> We must let art help us.
>
> ALICE WALKER, *The Same River Twice*

## What Is This Book About?

This is a book about using drama to create learning and change with
adolescents. It investigates a theatre arts education that guides students
to create and perform their own plays. This book presents and defines
five stages we have observed our students move through in classrooms
and theatre:

1. Using the Receptive Mind
2. Forming an Ensemble
3. Creating
4. Rehearsing
5. Performing

*Stages* refers here to floating and often interchangeable platforms of
learning as opposed to rigorously ordered steps, each a prerequisite to
another.

These five stages also organize our presentation here. Each chapter
includes academic essays, classroom activities, and interviews between
the authors and with students. As we honor a variety of learning styles
in our classrooms, we present the information in our book from several
perspectives to welcome a variety of readers.

Since theatre exercises form the framework of any performing arts
program, this book sets this framework into a larger learning structure
to build original performances out of students' lives. In this kind of

theatre, students find a safe place to learn, teachers work together to teach, and all can ensure that young voices are heard. Throughout the book, readers will see us inquiring into our own ways of learning, through our own common interests as well as ways of pursuing learning for all members of our classrooms.

Most teacher research has given us the model of a solitary teacher working to engage students as self-assessors in the learning process. Other models place teachers in a network of teaching professionals who share an interest in educational research, but seldom share school sites or even academic disciplines. In yet a third teacher-researcher model, the college or university researcher joins forces with his or her graduate students, who then write up the results of their classroom research in conjunction with a specific graduate studies program. These models, while helpful and interesting, failed to provide guidance for the teacher-to-teacher relationship: two classroom teachers discovering ways to teach by observing one another at work.

Because writing the book and designing a model of teacher research both qualify as acts of creation, it made sense to us early on to follow the same stages of learning we help our students follow. Participating in teacher-to-teacher research means a commitment to think critically about our own learning, a difficult task as individual performing arts teachers. Teachers do not often enjoy the freedom to sit off to the side, watch students, and reflect on their own methods. With two of us working together, one could be teaching and the other observing, and at the end of the day we could look back at what we had done. This book is a formal version of our look over each other's shoulders and a record of what we have learned by looking.

## How Did We Write This Book?

We offer here a basic outline of our methods of working together—Jan in St. Paul, Minnesota, and Jennifer in San Francisco, California. We revisit this topic in greater depth in both Chapter 5, Performing, and in the appendices. While visiting a youth arts center in Chicago in the summer of 1993, Jennifer was approached by a college intern who said, "If you like what you see here you should check out a Central Touring Theater in St. Paul. There's a teacher there who has kids write their own plays and tour them." She wrote down Jan's phone number, and Jennifer arranged a week-long visit in Jan's classroom.

We spent two years after that first visit getting to know each other as teachers and people before we began writing the book. Jennifer flew out to Jan's school site in St. Paul for week-long visits every other month. We scheduled these visits over the entire school year so that Jennifer could observe the various stages of creating plays the students performed. Each year Jan's advanced acting class doubles as a touring company, Central Touring Theater, which creates an original play and tours it throughout their community and the surrounding Midwest. This movement beyond the classroom or local school stage added dimensions to Jennifer's observations.

While observing Jan's classes in beginning, intermediate, and advanced acting, Jennifer sat off to the side, taking field notes by hand, and collected written work. From time to time she helped out with small chores such as photocopying, typing, answering phones, or chaperoning a field trip bus. For Jan, it was business as usual—teaching the class and running the touring company. She allowed time in her daily lessons for students to be interviewed by Jennifer and brought in former students, guest artists, and local educators, for interviews. When Jennifer had questions during class, Jan would more often than not refer her to a student for the answer. Jan did not edit what was happening in the class for Jennifer: Observations took place on good days and bad. At night, Jan would plan her lessons for the next day and Jennifer would type up her field notes. Together we would find an hour or two to discuss the events of the day and reflect on how to communicate what we were involved in to others.

During the next summer we spread data from the year out in front of us. This data included

> field notes from the classroom
> transcripts from the classroom
> audiotapes of interviews
> videos of performance work
> our own journals
> lesson plans
> student assignments
> play scripts written by students
> books about theatre and learning
> student journals

In this information we looked for patterns by which to organize our ideas. The five stages—Receptive mind, ensemble, creating, rehearsal, and performance—emerged early, and we then used them to organize the remainder of our work.

When we began to write, we sat at a computer and experimented with formats to describe the theatre exercises. From there, Jan took over collecting and writing the exercises and Jennifer began writing the essays. The sidebars throughout this book are direct student quotes. Those not attributed to a student are Jan's thoughts. Jennifer's observations of Jan's classes ended when she returned to teaching, but we continued to discuss lessons, share resources, keep written records, and travel back and forth during vacations to write.

## What Is Our Philosophy of Teaching?

The following outline of thirteen pedagogical principles that guide our teaching ends the introduction. We offer them not as commands or even advice, but as a means of defining who we are as educators. These principles also form the foundation of the work we examine in the following chapters.

### Successful theatre classes are organized.

- We distribute course outlines to students and parents and also use them to evaluate student and teacher progress.
- We publish lesson plans in step-by-step lead sheets organized in a binder available to all, monthly calendars, and sequential plans written on the board.

### Successful teachers come to class prepared, but also prepared to change in the moment.

- We keep a collection of activities that have worked well in the past near at hand in index card files and binders (see the exercises in each chapter).
- We keep a small library of books with exercises nearby (see the Annotated Bibliography).
- We view student tension, lack of energy, boredom, and discomfort with the topic as potential reasons for switching gears.

### Ensemble theatre work asks students to be able to work comfortably and equally with everyone in the group.

- We structure exercises so that students frequently change partners.
- We tell students to find partners with whom they do not normally work.
- We tell students to find partners by counting off, pairing up by height, color of clothing, or birth month.

***Successful teachers establish an active presence in the classroom and enjoy working with students.***

- We lead warm-ups by doing them.
- We come to class dressed to move comfortably.
- We risk looking silly.

***Even though it seems contradictory, the act of setting and enforcing time limits helps students to create.***

- We believe students accomplish as much or more by diving in and trying as by sitting and planning.
- We set a time limit at the beginning of an exercise, announce it or write it down for all to see, and enforce it even in the face of opposition.
- We put students in charge of watching the clock to share the responsibility of time limits.

***Communicating commands quickly and clearly is important in improvisational theatre.***

- We use the following signals to get students' attention during fast-paced work: striking a few beats on a drum, turning the lights on and off, blowing a whistle, playing a chord on the piano, lifting hands into the air, knocking a rhythm on a desk, or borrowing a student's loud voice.

***Teachers increase student success by relieving pressures of solo performance.***

- We direct scenes to rehearse or even perform at the same time.
- We use the noise of simultaneous performance as comforting insulator and atmospheric energizer.
- We have students perform in a larger space or out of doors, with the lights out, or with closed eyes.

***Students' voices constitute the central resource in a performing arts classroom.***

- We check the clock and ask, "How much time are we spending talking versus the students?" We invite colleagues, interns, and administrators to help watch for this balance.
- We design lessons in which we leave the room or do not speak at all.

- We take time to observe and record on tape or in notes what students are doing and saying.

### Students must feel ownership of the play they will be performing.

- We hold students responsible for choosing a play topic, creating the script, and performing the finished piece.
- We hold ourselves as teacher-directors responsible for designing and teaching the process, making editorial decisions with an eye on appropriateness, and setting and enforcing guidelines.
- We present these role definitions at the beginning of the process and repeat them throughout.

### Curriculum is discipline.

- We do not kick students out of class; doing so runs counter to the definition of the ensemble.
- We make discipline problems part of the warm-ups, acting exercises, group discussion, and reflection.
- We offer clear consequences such as time-outs, lost points, conferences, written examinations of incidents, or apologies.

### Some students use drama as a means for attracting unhealthy attention.

- We believe that the ensemble expects the teacher to redirect and control indulgent uses of drama by shifting activities, incorporating the problem into the play, or intervening with resources outside the classroom.

### Teachers who teach the arts participate in the arts.

- We try to take classes, keep a journal, attend plays and movies, write, and perform.
- We view time committed to nurturing the artistic spirit as time spent preparing for teaching.
- We share our creative work with students.

### Creating original plays reveals exciting success; it also produces failure.

- We accept that each original play takes participants into the unknown.

- We present failures to students as challenges rather than reasons to quit.
- We remember that the failures that are most discouraging in the moment lead to the greatest learning in the end.
- We try to laugh as much as possible.

# CHAPTER ONE

# The Receptive Mind

The pupil is out to receive [a] . . . humanistic
education, aimed not at imparting knowledge of the
literature, the history of theatre and so on, but at
awakening his sensibility.

JERZY GROTOWSKI, *Towards a Poor Theatre*

## Opening the Receptive Mind

The creative performing arts enable students to move through five essential, often overlapping, stages of learning:

[5 stages of learning]

1. Using the receptive mind
2. Becoming a productive member of an ensemble
3. Creating original work
4. Using the rehearsal process
5. Performing what has been created

These stages engage students simultaneously as performers, spectators,
artists, and critics.

## Defining the Receptive Mind

The receptive mind pervades all stages of the performing arts and is prerequisite to any kind of learning. A year into our research, Jan and I
each hung a series of five posters outlining these five stages of learning
for our drama students. My poster defining the receptive mind reads
like this:

*If You Have a Receptive Mind You Can . . .*
- Participate Enthusiastically
- Stop and Think About What Is Going On
- Be a Good Audience
- Concentrate and Stay Focused
- Keep Yourself Open to New Ideas

*open to new knowledge*

The receptive mind is a ready mind—ready to welcome the challenge that comes with taking on new knowledge. It is confident and willing and curious, without being overly judgmental. The receptive mind concentrates on a task for productive lengths of time, even through distractions. The receptive mind thinks about what is going on and how effects come about. The receptive mind carries on conversations with itself: pondering, trying out, and critiquing. Rather than a mind that contains a certain type of intelligence, it is a mind that knows when to use the many different intelligences it contains.

*Receptive mind is...*

With this concept, we move away from a focus on ability, assessing what a student can and cannot learn, and toward a focus on willingness, assessing when a student is ready to learn. The inherent assumption is that true learners do what another asks when they are sufficiently ready and prepared. As an English teacher, I customarily hear statements about how a student "cannot do" English. Honors, college prep, and remedial class tracking; reading-level tests; and subject-specific learning disabilities become the field's way to distinguish between those who can and cannot learn. Early in a child's education we allow for the possibility that a child must be ready to learn how to read or write, but when a student arrives in high school, readiness loses viability.

*Focus on whether student is ready/willing to learn*

In talking with and listening to colleagues, I often hear teachers express disappointment that they have to teach students how to learn before they teach them what to learn. Older colleagues feel this was not the case when they began teaching; as time has progressed, students have been arriving to school less and less prepared to do well. Younger colleagues admit that the methodology they were offered in credential programs focused on teaching subject matter in creative and comprehensive ways. And all teachers worry about the time teaching learning takes away from teaching required curricula.

> *I was hanging out with the guys, getting drunk, getting high, playing with guns. It was kind of uncomfortable. But it was also natural for me, because that's how I grew up. But when I came into theatre, it was something different. It was being productive, coming out of myself to create something that I can see and that other people can see. To tell people, "This is how I feel. This is what my mind creates."*
>
> *Ahanti, graduate of Central Touring Theater*

We have felt these concerns along with our colleagues and realize that our discipline makes a special way for receptive mind instruction. In a participation class, it is impossible to ignore when students are not receptive to what is being taught. We cannot wait for a test score to tell us how well our ideas are received. If students do not try when we ask them, the class cannot proceed. So, we design lessons to cover both the skills and the theories of our discipline as well as the tools for acquiring them. It is this practice, as opposed to setting aside a separate time for study skills or skipping them altogether, that accounts for the high participation and learning rate I see in Jan's class, and the higher rate I see in my drama, rather than my English classes.

To help ourselves understand how the receptive mind is engaged, Jan and I asked each other how we know when a student is using a receptive mind in class. We came up with a series of continua on which we hope to see students, and ourselves, balanced.

A Student Is Using a Receptive Mind When Balanced Between

| | | |
|---|---|---|
| Volunteering to participate | ←——→ | Encouraging others to participate |
| Creating spontaneously and trusting intuition | ←——→ | Making careful choices |
| Showing a fun, silly, energetic side | ←——→ | Showing a quiet, reflective, observant side |
| Taking care to present self well to others | ←——→ | Operating free of self-conscious restraints |
| Articulating opinions clearly | ←——→ | Listening respectfully to divergent opinions |
| Being comfortable on stage | ←——→ | Accepting uncomfortable moments as part of learning |
| Staying focused over extended periods | ←——→ | Transitioning smoothly between activities |
| Recognizing individual learning preferences | ←——→ | Using a variety of learning styles and intelligences |

## Observing the Receptive Mind *Encourage in order to foster recep mind*

Jan believes the single most important thing she can do to foster receptive minds is to ensure that a classroom environment is as encouraging

*take risks*

as possible. A receptive mind carries a willingness to try. Convincing students that they will not be singled out, made fun of, or expected to get it right the first time goes a long way toward convincing them to try something new. Exercises in this chapter offer strategies for getting past notions of a classroom as a place of judgment.

*get past classroom judgment*

Exercises such as Changing Partners Warm-Up, and Scene Starts in a Circle involve all students participating at once, whether they are asked to close their eyes, walk around the room, or talk to someone they do not know well all at the same time. More frequently than not, everyone simultaneously stands up to rehearse a piece to keep anyone from being singled out (in fact, the student not participating is the one likely to feel isolated), creating an instant need for concentration.

*All participate at same time*

A further demand on student concentration is the constant use of teacher coaching. Each activity shown here lists a few suggested coachings, but in the classroom, the coaching comes almost continuously, as reminders, further instructions, praise, and guidelines. Students know to listen, and while listening they train themselves to focus on the task at hand.

*Teacher Coaching*

*✳ Mind learning is physical*

Much of this receptive *mind* learning, paradoxically, is *physical* in nature—walking quickly around the room, lying on the floor, playing tag, dancing. We teach students not to sit and think too long, but to get up and give it a try and see what happens. Exercises such as Characters from the Freeze and Frozen Sculptures show that body positions can inspire dialogue, a hand-slap can be a way to meet a new person, and motions can communicate emotion.

Even as these exercises enhance learning through body movement, they also train students to stop moving to increase their learning. The command to freeze is a common one; it asks that students try absolute stillness ("Freeze even your eyes," Jan tells them) and remain that way for a specified period of time, considering what has just happened and listening to the coachings. The freeze is a multipurpose tool for building a receptive mind that

> fosters focus
> encourages metacognitive thinking
> promotes the idea of staying "in character"
> guides students through transitions
> offers the teacher time to evaluate

The receptive mind classroom alternates between encouraging its students to take new risks and lowering the level of risk in activities.

Even with the relaxation exercises, which stress the need for a quiet atmosphere, the teacher's voice is talking and guiding throughout. In this case the voice is quiet and slower, but still present, offering not only directions to follow ("If something is bothering you, notice it and then let it go") but also a running narrative of what is happening ("Follow your breath from your mouth to your lungs and back out again"). This running dialogue keeps students focused on the relaxation as a specific task, with its own demands and goals, rather than just an opportunity to lie around and daydream. Teacher narration also models the kind of metacognitive, thinking-about-two-things-at-once receptive mind approach that good thinkers and learners use.

During my second week of observations in Jan's classroom, I saw a beginning acting class taught the first period of the day that was rich in examples of receptive mind instruction. It was two and a half months into the school year, and the students were working on scene construction for the first time.

## FIELD NOTE EXCERPT: JAN'S CLASSROOM

### Scene Starts in a Circle Exercise

7:40–7:50 AM    Scene Construction

Jan quietly reaches behind her to turn off the music, and when it is silent she instructs kids to "drop your heads and close your eyes" and listen to her instructions. When their heads come up they will perform a line they hear at home frequently. They should try to make the performance as convincing as possible. The line should be short, and there will be no interruptions between lines. They are aiming at creating a "vocal collage" that will move fluidly around the circle. They are given time to think of a line, then instructed to turn so they are facing the outside of the circle and rehearse their lines to themselves, without yet concerning themselves with their neighbor's performance.

After less than a minute, they turn back into the circle and stand quietly, waiting for Jan's instruction to start. The students are quiet and focused on Jan. Once they begin, they have fun acting out parents and children with lines like, "Get off the phone, please!" or "I'll be back by dinner" or "Turn that stereo

Vocal Collage: Home dialogue

*I don't give a tremendous amount of feedback for a reason, because with students, they are used to waiting for approval from teachers: "Am I OK? Did I do it right?" There's a student in my class the other day who came in in tears: "My teacher didn't like my poem because the end of the poem didn't rhyme." In this class, I don't care if the end of your poems rhyme. It's not important. What I care about is that it's your voice. And if eventually you want the end of your poem to rhyme, we can work that out, but first I want to know how you feel.*

down this minute!" Students react in recognition of different lines, some meant to elicit a laugh ("Do you think you're going to wear that outfit to school young lady?") and some not ("You never listen to me"). Inbetween lines, Jan coaches, "Good! Keep it realistic. Be a respectful audience. Try not to play it for laughs."

**7:50–8:10 AM**

After creating this vocal collage, Jan splits the students into random groups of three. Jan repeats some of the lines performed in the circle and points out how they offer "automatic" conflicts: "Turn down that stereo this minute!" pits a music-enjoying teen against a silence-craving adult.

Five minutes are assigned for creating and rehearsing the scenes. Lights are turned up to full; the small groups spread out across the risers and get to work. The noise level is high, but as I walk around the room I hear only talk related to the task at hand. At the end of the five minutes, whether or not the students feel they are done, Jan instructs them to freeze in the position from which they will open their scenes. This freeze requires some coaching to make it last: "Exaggerate!" "Take a risk with your bodies." "Become someone else and stay in that character."

By my watch the students were expected to freeze for about ninety seconds. At Jan's verbal cue "Begin!" plus three thumps on a freestanding African drum at the base of the risers, the students simultaneously begin their performances. The room is loud with different groups performing conflicts between imaginary brothers, sisters, and parents. "FREEZE!" Jan thumps on the drum, and the students are surprised into a silence.

**8:10–8:15 AM**

Jan walks among the frozen groups and brings them one at a time to life by pointing and cueing "Go!" The group is expected to take up where they left off. Jan lets each scene run only for a few seconds before she refreezes the performers and points to the next group. Several of the groups enjoy the opportunity to perform and interject dramatic lines to evoke audience response. The audience is an obliging one, eager to vicariously relive familiar arguments. One scene with a mother, father, and son takes the class by surprise.

SON:     (*yelling*) You never listen to me!
MOTHER:  Well, we want to, dear, but you won't tell us what we want to know.
FATHER:  I'm not going to listen to you when you talk with that tone of voice.
SON:     See!
MOTHER:  What is it, son?
SON:     I'm gay!

The last line is delivered full front to the audience with falsetto voice tones. The mother in the scene screams and the father does a slapstick double take. The class erupts into laughter. Jan bangs on the drum: "Drop your heads!" she orders.

## 8:15–8:20 AM

The class is quiet. Jan walks through the room. "OK," she says. "I challenge you to go back and perform this scene for honesty, not for laughs." She asks a rapid-fire list of questions:

> What emotion is the father feeling under his gruffness?
> Does the mother already know what the son is going to say?
> How much courage does the son have to use to speak with his parents?

"A lot," one girl off to the side mutters under her breath.

While the performers are digesting this turn of events, Jan extends her challenge to the rest of the class. "Your job," she tells them, "is to support your classmates. They've chosen to do something very difficult, and it's your job to make this a safe place for them to take that risk."

*make safe space*

## 8:20–8:25 AM

Jan asks everyone not performing to sit down where they are and take a few deep breaths, then moves the performing group into the center of the room. On her command they freeze in the same opening position and perform the same improvised dialogue as before. But this time, the son delivers his final line hesitantly, looking quietly at the floor. The mother does not scream, and the father looks away. Jan stops the scene with a quiet "Freeze" command and the class is quiet for a few seconds before they applaud.

"Thank you," Jan says. "Didn't that feel more respectful?"

---

Just as evaluation scales can be used to assess the receptivity of a student's mind, they can also be used to assess how well a class or lesson plan allows for receptive mind instruction. The lesson described here is aimed at teaching a specific theater theory—how the establishment of Who, What, and Where is fundamental in scene construction—but reveals receptive mind instruction and expectations throughout. The class swings back and forth between an upbeat pace, with its loud, five-minute group rehearsals and abbreviated performances, and a quiet pace, with its freezes and mini-lectures by the teacher. Students participate singly and in groups; they work and watch. Jan goes to careful lengths to make the classroom as safe as possible, by providing clear

> *A receptive mind is a trusting mind. You have to have faith that we can bring the best of everybody out in a certain environment. I think if you don't have faith that a small group can work together, then how can you have faith that a family can work together, that the community can work together, that the world can work together?*

limits, and plenty of instruction, to let the class know that they are expected to check ridiculing behavior at the door, and for at least these fifty class minutes, treat one another respectfully.

The theme of respect resurfaces when Jan seizes an uncomfortable moment for learning purposes. She praises the group in the coming-out scene for trying, but ultimately does not accept their work. The students learn that it is OK to try something risky, and that redoing is a common expectation of learning. Their scene is also the final stage in a gradual progression from whole-group work to solo performance. At first the class performs in the circle, then simultaneously in groups of three; then finally, one group performs with the rest of the class seated as an audience.

Of all the receptive mind expectations, acceptance is prerequisite to the others. Without it, the classroom is not a safe space for learning. Students worry if others will make fun of them (and sometimes if they should make fun of others) instead of creating. In the preceding exercise, Jan is able, through her quick head-drop command, series of questions, and it-will-be-hard-but-you-can-rise-to-it challenge, to rebuild safety in the classroom within the exercise.

Even when classroom disputes cannot be solved this gently, it remains the teacher's responsibility to reinforce vigorously the expectation of respect in the classroom. Several months after the beginners' experience with the coming-out improvisation, Jan's advanced acting students have an argument about one student who has written the insult "faggot" into a scene he is writing for the upcoming playwriting festival. The class leaves in anger that day and returns the next day to a lecture from Jan.

---

## FIELD NOTE EXCERPT: CLASSROOM TRANSCRIPT

### Jan's Respect Discussion

JAN: Yesterday tensions were happening in here. It was kind of nice that they happened so that I can talk to you about a few things. I just want to bring it up and I don't want to make any big discussion about it actually. I want to set some expectations.

CLASS:    I don't want to talk about this.

Why do we have to talk about this?

Oh God.

JAN:    You guys, shhhh. I'm going to do this in about two minutes to reinforce some expectations that I have of what a safe space is about. In general a safe space is like a relationship; it's not something you get and then it's there all the time. It's something you have to work on.

*Safe Space*

As far as inside your plays, even though a character may really say a word like "faggot," I don't want derogatory language used in this classroom or in your plays without a discussion. If you use the word the way it was being used yesterday in some of the discussions, then no.

CLASS:    But—

Hey—

Wait—

JAN:    Hang on. And if you don't like this rule you can go and deal in another class, OK?

STUDENT 1:    That is censorship.

JAN:    And if you call that censorship, fine.

STUDENT 2:    She just means, don't say it and then go nowhere with it.

STUDENT 3:    If you leave that kind of language going nowhere in your scene then it comes out sounding like, A, that you feel that way because you wrote the play, and B, that the class feels that way because they performed it.

STUDENT 1:    So it has to mean something?

STUDENT 3:    And we don't want to just send the message that it's OK to use that language because we're in theater and we're special. That we can just go around using a negative word like *Spic* and then just say, "Oh, we didn't mean it!"

JAN:    I don't want us to hurt each other in here.

This exchange shows students and teacher struggling to balance on one of the essential scales of evaluation for the receptive mind:

Articulating opinions     ⟷     Listening respectfully to
clearly                                     divergent opinions

Jan again ends the class discussion on a positive note, but toes a harder line to get there. The student's complaint of "censorship" implies a commonly heard assumption that an art class is a place where anything should be allowed under the label of creativity. But the truth of the matter is that in order to teach students acceptance, and thereby foster the receptive mind, teachers themselves must be unaccepting of certain behaviors. Each teacher will draw the line in a different place, but as Jan's exchange above shows, clear statements about the expectations and consequences must occur. Here, restatement of the rule allows students to discuss why it is a good idea. More students agree with Jan than not, but the minority who do not agree initially silence the others with fear that they, too, will be treated disrespectfully. Jan's discussion extends permission to students to be respectful to one another.

## An Introduction to the Exercises

We would like to say a few words about the exercises in this book. Each chapter offers a collection of exercises designed to teach the chapter's concepts. Each collection begins with two or three pages of brief warm-up exercises and is followed by ten to twenty more formal exercises.

Each formal exercise begins with a brief description, lists any special considerations, provides a step-by-step procedure, and ends with variations for further exploration. Within these exercises we offer sample coachings (words we are likely to say to students that direct them throughout the activity). For a list of universal coachings that we find ourselves using in all the exercises, see Appendix Two.

## Receptive Mind Warm-Ups

*Warm-Ups for Introduction*

### CHAIR PLAY

Have a group of ten to twelve players sit in chairs in a circle, with one volunteer in the middle as IT. The object of the game is for IT to find a chair in which to sit. IT begins by walking around the circle slowly, asking each person, "May I sit in your chair?" Those sitting in the circle begin to make eye contact with one another, and on silent impulse, two people quickly exchange chairs. IT tries to sit in one of the empty chairs while the exchange is happening. Pairs in the outside circle should be changing chairs quickly and continuously. When the person in the middle gets a chair, the person without a chair is IT and the game continues.

### GROUPING

Call out a category and direct students to get in appropriate groups as quickly as possible. Example categories include

> clothing colors
> birth order (youngest, middle, oldest, or only child)
> favorite radio stations

Within each group have participants learn each others' names.

### WALK AND NOTICE

As students walk randomly around the room, coach them to observe their surroundings. Have them freeze, shut their eyes, and answer a few questions about the performance space. For example:

> Who is wearing a gray sweatshirt?
> How many lights are there on the ceiling?
> What poster is closest to the door?

> How many chairs are on the right side of the room?

Students call out answers. Then have them open their eyes, check it out for themselves, and resume walking and observing until the next freeze when they answer a different set of questions.

*Warm-ups for Communication*

## VOCAL MIRRORS

Have students face their partners. Partner A begins telling a story, speaking slowly and clearly. Partner B attempts to join in so they are saying the words together. On cue, partners reverse and Partner B initiates the story. Once students are successful at this exercise, have them both tell stories and listen at the same time. On cue have them attempt to repeat back the partner's story.

## TALKING ON TOPICS

Generate a list of topics. Have students walk around the room. Coach them to avoid eye contact with anyone and to create their own focus while moving among the group. Have them freeze and call out a topic or a phrase. Ask the students to continue walking and begin talking nonstop on a given topic, such as

| | |
|---|---|
| your neighborhood | friendship |
| television | homelessness |
| babies | homework |
| the environment | money |
| school lunch | family |

## TALK AND STOP

For this exercise, half the class lines up in a straight line and the other half watches. Select a topic. Ask the students in line to begin talking on that topic, nonstop. Everyone will be talking at once, looking straight out into the audience. The object is for everyone in the group to stop talking at the exact same time, but without the assistance of any cueing. Coach them to listen to each other and stop on impulse as a group.

*Warm-ups for Physicalization*

## PERSONALITY TAG

The person who is IT starts moving around the room with a unique character walk. The class copies IT and begins a game of tag. The next person tagged as IT introduces a new character walk and the game proceeds.

## WARM-UP ROTATION

Groups of five stand in small circles and number off. Person 1 in each group begins leading a physical warm-up and everyone follows. Next call out "Person 2" and that person takes the lead. Next call out "Freeze," and everyone freezes except Person 2, who leaves his group and quickly finds another group to lead. Keep calling out numbers to change the leaders. Call out "Freeze" to rotate leaders to their new groups. This rotation is a low-risk way of creating connections and breaking down group barriers. Music not only creates mood, but changing the music with each leader can inspire a variety of physical expression.

## RED LIGHT! GREEN LIGHT!

Play the traditional playground game Red Light! Green Light!, and each time players move call out an image for the students to physicalize. For example:

> Move like a spider.
> Now you are weightless in space.
> You are bowling balls.
> You are an ocean wave.
> You are slam-dunking a basketball.

*The body is also a receptacle of information and emotions. When we tell stories in a circle, I have them stand up and act the stories out. So much more comes out when they are moving. The fact is that the moving body can produce things. And in order to be able to endure and focus and concentrate, you need to be healthy and you need to have a functioning, healthy body. When kids start becoming aware of their bodies, they can be aware of when it's healthy and when it's not. This is also another alternative form of a "high" for kids. It's a healthy high.*

### *Warm-Ups for Focus*

## GO

The group stands in a circle. One person, A, points randomly to another person, B, who loudly says, "Go." Person A then moves to Person B's place while B points to C and says, "Go." Continue until everyone is involved. Coach for sustained eye contact and consistent rhythm of movement. For well-focused groups take away the word "Go" and proceed with the exercise nonverbally, simply pointing and moving.

## SOUND AND MOVEMENT ONE-TWO-THREE

Have students stand each facing a partner, and select a Partner A and Partner B. Ask pairs to count to three as many times as they can, alternating so that A says, "One," B says, "Two," A says, "Three," B says, "One," and so on. When a good level of concentration is achieved, pause the exercise. Have pairs replace the word "One" with a sound and movement, then continue counting with "Two" and "Three," striving to maintain the original counting rhythm. Pause the exercise, have students replace the word "Two" with a sound and movement, and begin counting again. Finally, instruct team to replace "Three" with a sound and movement, and count with sound and movements only, as many times as possible.

## MAKING CONNECTIONS

Have students sit in a tight circle. Ask for two volunteers to sit in the center, as close as possible, holding hands, and looking directly at each other. Each student must say, "I want you; I need you; I love you" sincerely, without breaking concentration. Have students take turns. Once students have mastered this challenge, they can be coached to add detail and justify their actions.

## MIRROR ART

Students work in partners, with a Person A and Person B. Person A, using an imaginary box of crayons, draws a picture in the air, and Person B mirrors Person A's work. Next, Person B, using real crayons and paper, draws what she perceives her partner to be drawing. Reverse roles and compare and contrast results. Coach for perception and observation; accuracy in the artwork is not important.

## WALK, FREEZE, FIND AN OBJECT

Have students move randomly around the space, and call out "Freeze." Describe to them an imaginary object that is on the floor near them, such as

| | |
|---|---|
| a large wooden door | a bike with a flat tire |
| an old book | a present in a big box |
| a bowl of cookie dough | two jars of finger paint |

Coach students to explore each object in detail, using all their senses. Finally, they can bring to life a character that evolves from their interaction with the object.

## WHOM DO YOU FEAR?

Have students move randomly around the room. Ask them each to secretly select someone in the room to "fear" and then to stay as far away from that person as possible. Next, ask them to silently select someone to be their "guardian" and to stay as close to them as possible. Working as an ensemble, students will continuously group and disperse. Close by having students point out whom they selected to fear or used to guard them. This can lead to a discussion on how fear isolates people into groups, and comfort keeps people from facing fears or taking risks.

### *Warm-ups for Writing*

## HOT TOPICS

A spontaneous way to generate a list of topics for creative work begins by having students form a circle. Have them toss a ball randomly around and across the circle. Ask each person, while holding the ball, to call out a theme or topic that is important to him or her or to the community, then toss the ball to the next player. Have a volunteer write all the suggestions on some butcher paper and keep them up in the room as reference for scene work or discussion.

## VISUALIZATION TO MUSIC

Have students sit alone and close their eyes. Play music that evokes images and emotions. Coach students to visualize mental pictures to the music, using all their senses. If students get stuck in the process, encourage them to focus on a detail or expand the image to a wide-angle view. After the visualization, have them write or draw what they saw.

### *Warm-ups for Characterization*

## OBJECTIVE AND OBSTACLES IMPROV

Working alone, have each student create a short silent moment that includes a character, a clear objective (or desire), and an obstacle. For example:

A child wants to get into her house but the key will not work.
A cook wants to cut an onion but cannot stand the smell.
A weight lifter wants to lift a weight, but cannot get it off the floor.

Remind students to communicate their specific environment through action and

*Intuition is important, and I think it's another thing you train kids to use. I have exercises that do that. I point it out to kids: "When you turned around and looked back and caught that person's eye, what motivated that?" Intuition. It's a connectedness that comes after paying attention for a long time, and knowing, and having repeated interactions with people that you know enough to do that.*

objects. Moments can be performed simultaneously or singled out for presentation.

## WATCHING WHAT?

Working in groups of five or six, each group agrees on an activity that they all will watch. For example:

| | |
|---|---|
| a tennis game | a cooking demonstration |
| a fight | an airplane crash |

One at a time, each group presents their watching activity, and the other groups try to guess what they are watching. For variety, direct students to use another sense, such as taste, touch, or smell.

## ENTER ANYWHERE

Define a place, such as a

| | |
|---|---|
| bus stop | park bench |
| doctor's office | ball park |

Have students enter the space as a character. Have them begin by participating in silence. Then add on speech and other character choices such as age, occupation, or attitude.

## BASIC IMPROV SCENE

Ask for two volunteers to stand up. Ask the class to define *who* these two characters will be, *where* they will be, and suggest a *conflict* that will connect them. Allow the two volunteers to begin the scene. Freeze them at a heightened moment and repeat the process, letting students generate ideas for scenes.

# Exercises for Teaching the Receptive Mind

## CHANGING PARTNERS WARM-UP

### Description

This exercise is structured so that students preview a variety of basic acting skills while changing partners continually to learn names and to make working connections with the group.

### Considerations

Upbeat instrumental music creates energy and motivation for this activity, which is done silently in partners.

### Procedure

1. With students in partners, assign an activity for two, such as

   *One person lifts an imaginary weight, while the partner is the spotter.*

2. Allow a short time for partners to complete the task, then coach them to partner up with someone new. Examples of partner tasks include:

   *Stare Down*: Students stand facing their partners, and begin a simple stare down, looking each other in the eyes, trying not to laugh. Coach for concentration. Conclude after about a minute.

   *Handshake*: Working with new partners, students create a three-part hand slap greeting, and rehearse until it is memorized.

   *Portrait Painter*: Again with new partners, one person is a portrait painter and the other is the model. Act out this interaction in pantomime.

3. Coach students through activities.

   *Basketball*: Partners are sixteen years old, playing one-on-one basketball on a very hot day.

   Work silently; show the activity with action, not words.
   See the colors of the paint.
   Show how you feel by the way you use your brush.
   What does it feel like to have to sit still for so long?
   Act out silently.
   Keep track of the imaginary ball.
   Feel the sun on your body.

> *Through working on the plays, I've come to understand that racism is one of the ugly spots on the human race. But outside of it lies hope, and if we use this, we can prevail over all.*
>
> *Jason, advanced acting student*

4. Continue to freeze and repartner students in various situations.
   *Variation 1: Rerun*
   Return to any scene or activity in any order and as many times
   as is productive. Add dialogue, gibberish, or passage of time.
   For example, return to the basketball player, adding twenty-
   five years to his age; or return to the portrait painter, adding
   arthritis to her hands and frustration to the model's attitude.

## SCENE STARTS IN A CIRCLE

### Description
This is a simple, low-risk acting exercise in which students work in
partners to create short scenes inspired by a familiar sentence.

### Considerations
It is helpful to have chairs and/or theatre boxes available.

### Procedure
1. Students stand in a circle.
2. Have students think of a phrase or saying that they often hear
   at home.

   Get your feet off the couch.
   Don't use that tone of voice with me, young lady.
   Have you done your homework yet?

3. On command, students perform their lines simultaneously.
4. Next students perform their individual lines and movements one
   at a time, with the rest of the class.
5. Divide the students into pairs. Each pair is given sixty seconds to
   create a brief scene that begins with one of their two lines.
6. At the teacher's direction, each pair performs their scene until the
   teacher stops them. Keep the performances *very brief*—ten seconds is plenty for the scene to peak.
   *Variation 1: Student-Generated Topic*
   Have students change partners and select their own topic.
   *Variation 2: Frozen Start*
   Still working in partners, have students create frozen sculptures
   and ask the group to define a Who, a What, and a Where, and
   bring these frozen moments to life for a brief interaction.
   *Variation 3: Multiple Endings*
   Select one of the scenes to focus on. Have all the groups come
   up with different endings to refocus the scene.

## CIRCLE STORIES ON THE MOVE

### Description
A takeoff on the familiar story-pass game during which a group story is composed; this version adds physical and characterization elements.

### Procedure
1. Have students sit in small group circles of six to eight.
2. Tap one student on the shoulder; this student becomes the story-teller and begins telling an imaginary story.
3. At the teacher's direction, the storyteller points to someone in the circle who then continues the same story from the exact point where the first storyteller left off. Coach for cooperation.

   Listen to each other.
   Take over the story without pausing or repeating words.

4. For round two, everybody stands up. This time, the person tapped begins not only telling an imaginary story, but physically acting out the motions of the story as well. Coach for performance.

   Physically exaggerate actions and emotions.
   Include your face in the action, too.
   Use all of the space around you.

5. The rest of the circle members simultaneously mirror the physical actions of the storytellers, so that all group members are participating in the physicalization of the story. On cue, the teller points to a new teller and the game proceeds.
6. For round three, assign each student a character who will tell the story, for example:

   preacher       cheerleader       military sergeant

## SIMULTANEOUS MONOLOGUES

### Description
Here students apply the skills of speaking, listening, and characterization learned in Circle Stories on the Move to a performance exercise.

### Procedure
1. Two students stand side-by-side facing the audience. Give them a common, shared experience that they must talk about simultaneously. For example:

   A waiter and a customer remember a bad interaction at a restaurant.

A parent and child remember a night when the child came home very late.

Two siblings retell an argument they had after dinner last night.

2. Direct students to tell this imaginary story to the audience from their point of view, as a monologue. They should also be listening to their partner and integrating words and phrases from their partner's story into their own.

3. Coach students to talk continuously without pausing to listen to their partner, and to continue speaking and working with their partner to unfold the details of the story being created.

## DEFINING WHO, WHAT, AND WHERE

### Description
This is a short, low-risk improvisation exercise in which students work as partners to focus on establishing the Who, What, and Where in a scene.

### Procedure
1. Have the class sit or stand in two lines, Line A and Line B, facing one another.

2. The first person from Line A enters the playing space and begins an activity with a pantomimed object.

washing dishes       fishing       playing basketball

3. The first person from Line B enters the playing space and begins a spoken, improvised scene with Person 1. Together in the scene, the two players must establish the Who (who the characters are

*Who, What, Where*

and what their relationship is to one another); the What (the nature of the activity with the object); and the Where (the location in which the activity is taking place).

PERSON 1:   Begins by pantomiming washing dishes. (*What*)
PERSON 2:   Mom, I'm sorry I forgot about the dishes; I know it was my night to do them. (*Who*)
PERSON 1:   That's OK. Get out of the kitchen. You can also forget about your allowance for this week. (*Where*)

4. Listen for the Who, What, and Where in a scene; once you identify these elements, stop the scene and call up the next two line members, who repeat the exercise creating a new object and scene.
5. The game continues until everyone has had a turn. For a second round, switch the roles of the lines, so that Line B supplies the object and Line A supplies the improv beginning. Allow the students who are watching to identify the elements as they see them.

## FOUR SQUARE TRANSFORMING EMOTIONS

### Description
This is a game played entirely in silence, in which students pantomime activities with objects while motivated by a series of emotions.

### Procedure
1. Divide the room into four parts, or squares, each of which is identified by an emotion:

| | |
|---|---|
| anger | joy |
| depression | excitement |

2. Divide the class into four equal groups, and have each stand in one square of the room.
3. Assign each group an activity.

| | |
|---|---|
| digging a ditch | washing a floor |
| playing in a band | building a sand castle |

4. Have each group begin the assigned activity in the emotion dictated by the square.
5. On cue, students move clockwise as quickly as possible to the next square, continuing their original activity, but now in the emotion of the second square. For example, if they began washing the floor angrily, then they move to washing the floor joyfully. Coach students through transitions..

*Four Square Transforming Emotions*

Maintain eye contact with people in your group.
Use nonverbal conversation.
Give weight to the objects with which you are working.
Try to keep objects the same size.
Show how you are feeling by the way you handle the objects.
Work with your group, not by yourself.
Move as quickly as you can from one square to the next—run!

6. Keep students moving from one square to the next until energy
   peaks.
   *Variation 1: Transforming Activity*
   Have the squares labeled by activity, and have students maintain the same emotion throughout.
   *Variation 2: Scene Start-up*
   Isolate one character and activity—for example, a hyper person
   in a band, or a depressed person digging a hole—as the starting
   point of a scene.

*Variation 3: Four Actor Four Square*
The same activity is performed by four individuals, rather than groups, while the audience watches and gives feedback.

## RAMBO, TEXAS

### Description
The following exercise was developed by actor T. Mychael Rambo who collected more than thirty old black-and-white portraits of family members dating back to the late 1800s and early 1900s in the town of Rambo, Texas. Personal photo albums are a rich source for creative writing, emotional recall, and character development.

### Procedure
1. Gather students together and show them a series of carefully selected photographs.
2. Display the photos around the room and let students wander and look.
3. Ask students to select one picture and study it for a few minutes.
4. Direct students to write a poem or monologue inspired by the picture.
5. When they are finished, ask students to read or perform their piece to the group. Pass around their picture during this time.
6. Encourage feedback and discussion with coaching.

   What specifically inspired your writing?
   What drew you to your picture?
   Whose writing affected or moved you? Why?
   How can this exercise be helpful to a playwright? To an actor?

   *Variation 1: Personal Photo Search*
   Have students go through their own picture albums and select a picture that brings back a significant memory or awakens a strong emotion. Ask them to write a poem or monologue based on the picture and share it with the class.
   *Variation 2: Art Project*
   Glue writing and picture on a piece of paper, decorate it, and hang it up in the space for decoration.
   *Variation 3: Bring a Photo to Life*
   Select a photograph with three to five people in a dramatic action pose. Have students study the characters and bring them to life in a scene beginning or ending in that identical pose.

*Characters from the Freeze*

## CHARACTERS FROM THE FREEZE

### Description
Ask students to create characters out of shapes spontaneously formed by their bodies.

### Considerations
Playing a variety of music during this exercise helps participants let go of thoughts and inhibitions. This allows the body, rather than the mind, to reveal solutions and information.

1.  Have students move around the room following a series of directions.

    Move through space quickly.
    As you move, make your body as large or as small as you can.
    Move large and fast; express the emotion of joy.
    Move small and in slow motion; express the emotion of fear.
    When the music gets louder, move more quickly.
    Move your torso, your shoulders, your face.

2.  When the group is physically loose and emotionally open call out, "Freeze." Instruct students to concentrate on the frozen position of their bodies, and let their shapes inform them of a character.

3.  Suggest an activity for their characters to perform, such as cleaning the house or packing a suitcase. Or, allow them to begin an activity with an object of their choice, such as brushing their hair or painting a picture. Coach them to detail the character as they work.

    Give this character a name, an age.
    What words would describe this character's personality?
    What does this character love to do?
    Make this a special day in this character's life.
    Is this day wonderful or deeply stressful?

How is this character feeling?
Show this feeling in your body and in
your actions.

4. If their concentration allows, instruct
   students to begin softly speaking the
   inner thoughts of the character, in a
   quiet, stream-of-consciousness monologue. It is important to encourage
   them to continue the activity as they
   speak.
5. This can be repeated so students can
   generate a variety of characters.
6. In conclusion, have them pick their
   favorite character and write a short
   poem or monologue. If time allows,
   have them read their work to a
   partner.

*If you understand healthy
adolescent development, there are
things that you might do that
would not look right to somebody
who doesn't understand what
you're doing, but it works for kids.
There is an artistry to that. There's
this piece about life story, that all
of us are doing our own story, and
theatre is about that. It's wonderful
to recognize that in shaping stories
we make connections with people,
in human ways, caring ways,
respectful ways, fun ways.*

Mary Burnison, Youth Studies
Department, University
of Minnesota

## FROZEN SCULPTURES

### Description
Here scenes and characters are generated from physical and visual
work. Small groups create frozen moments of action that become inspiration for creation.

### Procedure
1. Divide students into small groups.
2. Select a motivating theme, such as

   courage      escape to freedom      falling in love      curiosity

3. On cue, instruct students to create a physical picture of the theme
   word in a short span of time, say ten seconds, without talking.
   They can create the sculpture one at a time, building on each
   other's moves, or just quickly create a frozen pose working together as a group. Encourage contact and physical connections.
4. Have students hold the frozen moment by actively coaching.

   Support your own weight.
   Keep the feelings running through your body.
   Maintain a strong body position.
   Make eye contact and heighten connections with the group.

5. Release students from the sculpture or have them maintain the pose and extend the activity using a variation below.

*Variation 1: Memory Work*
After creating a sculpture, have students leave the sculpture slowly in eight counts, freeze for a moment, then return back slowly in eight counts and freeze in the original pose as accurately as possible.

*Variation 2: Bring It to Life*
Have the class mill around one statue and suggest a variety of interpretations of the image. Actors in the sculpture can be described as characters or inanimate objects. Select one interpretation and have the actors bring that moment to life, in slow motion, in silence, or with words.

*Variation 3: Beginnings and Endings*
Have students commit the frozen moment to memory. Instruct them to create an improvisational scene that either begins or ends with that exact frozen moment. It can include dialogue or be entirely in pantomime.

*Variation 4: Stop Action Story Statues*
Working in small groups, students create a story by crafting a series of frozen moments inspired by a given theme. Transitions from one statue to the next should be quick and deliberate and have a beginning, middle, and end. Add live drums or recorded music to drive and heighten the mood and action.

## SILENT SCULPTURES

### Description
Students work in silence, creating sculpted moments of human interaction. Sculptures can then become starting points for scenes, characters, and other creative activities.

### Procedure
1. Students work in partners. Person A is the sculptor and Person B acts as human clay and is sculpted into a frozen moment.
2. In this version, Person A, the sculptor, must communicate and shape the frozen moment nonverbally. Sculptors can position themselves exactly how they want their sculptures to be and allow their partners to try to match it, or they can gently and respectfully position their partners' bodies to achieve the most accurate image.

Take your time.
Create a shape or a character and let your partner try to match it.

*Silent Sculpting*

Detail the expressions.
Take risks with the positions.
Be respectful as you shape each other's bodies.
Experiment with different poses until you reach the desired effect.

3. Students being sculpted are to remain cooperative and reflect the images demonstrated by their sculptors. They may require encouragement to maintain frozen positions with commitment.
4. Have students take turns sculpting with different partners.
   *Variation 1: Create a Story*
   When sculptures are completed, sculptors can walk around the spaces as if it were a wax museum or sculpture garden and observe the images. Students can try to create stories attached to each piece.
   *Variation 2: Create a Picture*
   Ask students to observe all the sculptures and select several that seem to have some sort of connection. Place them on stage in a deliberate arrangement. Ask students to describe and define the frozen moments suggested by the sculptures.

*Variation 3: Create a Scene*
Have students work in groups of four. One person becomes the sculptor and shapes the other three into a frozen moment in a scene. These moments can be brought to life using slow motion, sound, gibberish, or words.

## MOVING MEDITATION

### Description
The song "Sankofa" by Cassandra Wilson was first used to set the tone for this relaxation exercise. This song describes the journey of a mystical African bird that rose up from the flames of despair and was born anew.

### Considerations
A piece of relatively simple, soulful music that could inspire a wide range of feeling is essential in setting the mood. Lowered lighting is also helpful.

### Procedure
1. Have students stand with eyes closed, breathing deeply through their entire bodies to relaxation.
2. Play the music selection. Coach students to listen closely to the melody, lyrics, and instruments in the piece. Encourage them to be affected emotionally by the music rather than judging it intellectually.
3. Ask students to focus their attention on their right hand, letting it fill up with the music and with emotion. Then coach them to allow the hand to "dance" independently, moving freely, as if it has a life of its own.
4. Now have students add the left hand, allowing it its own expression and movements.
5. Coach students to add other body parts, each independent of the other, until the whole body is moving.

   Move each part slowly, staying connected to the music.
   Take risks.
   Look for new ways to explore space around you.
   Work to avoid repetition.
   Open your eyes when you can do so without passing judgment.
   Allow your body to express itself through shape, form, and movement.
   Trust your impulses—be spontaneous.

6. As the music ends, instruct students to begin moving in slow motion until they are standing still, again with their eyes closed, reflecting on the experience and how they feel.

## MEAL MIRRORS

### Description
Students work in partners. One person pantomimes an improvisation while the other becomes a mirror and reflects every action.

1. Pair students: Person A is the mover and Person B is the mirror. Coach the mover to select a character and cook dinner as that person.

   How old are you?
   What is your name?
   Who are you cooking this meal for?
   Smell the food.
   What else is on your mind besides dinner?
   Show how you feel by how you use the objects.
   What are you wearing?
   What are you cooking?

2. Instruct Person B to observe Person A preparing the meal, and on command, Person B attempts to mirror their actions. Because Person A will be moving quickly, the focus for Person B is not to mirror the actions precisely, but to mirror the essence of the actions and the changing emotions.

   Reflect the actions and the emotions of your partner.
   Try to guess what your partner is cooking.
   Imagine what your partner might be thinking.
   Observe and integrate details of personality.
   Do not add your own moves; strive for unity with your partner.

3. If energy is low, impose a time limit with coaching, such as

   It's getting late and your guest will be here in one minute.

4. At the conclusion of the piece, ask the mirrors to describe in detail what they learned about the character they followed. Encourage both partners to discuss the differences and similarities in their perceptions.

5. Repeat the exercise, this time with Person B cooking breakfast.

## CONCENTRATION GAME

### Description

The objective of this activity is for students to maintain concentration while trying to eliminate others from the scene by making them laugh.

### Procedure

1. Select five volunteers.
2. Establish an imaginary environment on stage by pointing out boundaries and indicating any objects inside of it.

   a laundromat with washers, benches, doors, counters
   a classroom with desks, board, windows, clock

3. Coach each volunteer to enter the environment, one at a time, in character and create an improvised scene.

   Create a character who is different from yourself.
   Bring an imaginary object in with you.
   What is your character's reason for being here?
   Try to eliminate others in the scene by making them laugh.
   Don't break character. Hold your concentration.
   Keep interacting with others on stage.
   Don't hide your face.

4. Students are eliminated from the scene when they break character or laugh.
5. Actors may not touch or tickle in their attempts to break each other's concentration.
6. The last character on stage "wins" the round.
   *Variation*
   Hold students responsible for remembering the order in which they were eliminated. Then replay the game, but this time with all of the people who were eliminated first, second, third, or last improvising together.

## SOUND CIRCLE

### Description

Sound Circle is a small-group activity stressing relaxation, listening, and ensemble development through the task of creating a collage of vocal sounds.

### Procedure

1. Seat six to eight students in a tight circle in the middle of the room with eyes closed; the rest of the class observes quietly.
2. Tap one student on the shoulder. This student creates a vocal sound with a consistent rhythm that can be repeated for the duration of the exercise.
3. Allow a few seconds for the first student to become comfortable with his/her sound.
4. The second student tapped creates a unique repeatable vocal sound. As in singing a round or improvising jazz, the second student fits his or her sound into a repeatable pattern with the first sound.
5. Each student fits a new sound into the circle when tapped.
6. All students concentrate on consistently maintaining the sound circle.

> Sometimes I use what I've learned in drama in my other classes. But it's harder, because a lot of teachers don't allow that. They feel like they have to be the person always in charge. Even though Jan is the person in charge the students are helping, helping as one. It's harder for me to concentrate when other people aren't helping me.
>
> Shawn, intermediate acting student

Conclusion 1

When students are tapped a second time, they stop making their sound, thereby gradually and rhythmically disassembling the circle.

Conclusion 2

The teacher uses vocal commands to conduct the circle once everyone is participating; for example, she can instruct the students to go faster, slower, louder, softer, or fade out.

Conclusion 3

The teacher uses a tap system to communicate the following commands: two taps = stop; one tap = begin a new sound to conduct new collages.

# CHAPTER TWO

# The Ensemble

Equal participation is, of course, the cornerstone of most classrooms. This notion usually involves everything except free play, which is generally considered a private matter. Yet, in truth, free acceptance in play, partnerships, and teams is what matters most to any child. *Team Acceptance*

VIVIAN GUSSIN PALEY, *You Can't Say You Can't Play*

## Defining Ensemble

### FIELD NOTE EXCERPT: JENNIFER'S CLASSROOM

#### The Mushroom Exercise

I was introducing Sylvia Plath's poem "Mushrooms" to my sophomore English class. When students walked into the room on this day, they saw their desks facing one another in groups of four, with each group sporting its own collection of shitake, lobster, morel, and button mushrooms; mushroom identification books; collections of pictures from fairy tales featuring mushrooms; and dictionaries open to the mushroom page. I felt sure this activity would be the one to finally succeed with this hard-to-motivate class.

For this day I was assigning students to groups, using name tags to indicate who was to sit with whom. As they came in the door, students did initially allow their curiosity to surface: "I hate mushrooms!" "An orange mushroom?" "What's this?" Students walked around the desks, poking at the mushrooms and looking for their name tags. When almost everyone was settled, one last student walked into the room and located her seat for the day. "Him?" She asked in a loud tone to the class at large. Then she looked right at me, "I can't work with him. Everyone knows I don't like him."

I did not know what to do. It was hard for me to accept that a student could be so mean-spirited to a classmate in a room that was supposed to be under my control. The class was silent, looking at me. Their expectant faces told me that they believed that the two would not be made to sit together after such a boldly rude comment. I asked the first question that came to my mind, "What's wrong with him?" She was silent, then she tossed her hair in exasperation, "Whatever."

---

At first this behavior was shocking to me, because I saw it as evidence that a student was willing to do whatever she could, no matter how hurtful, in order to work with her friends. Now this behavior strikes me as more sad than shocking, because I see it as evidence of how frightening it can be for an adolescent to work with someone she did not know well. It is hard to remember, even when working with adolescents daily, how important social connections can be in the teenage world. For better or worse, they can define a young person's entire life, and this is the challenge that a teacher faces when setting out to teach students how to form and function as an ensemble. To teach ensemble drama is to force students to work together.

Theatre arts are, by definition, a group undertaking. As opposed to many of the fine arts, where one person can paint a picture or throw a pot, a play requires a playwright to imagine the idea, a director to interpret the words of the playwright to a cast of actors, and a host of technical creators to bring the vision together. By the time even a small play is "put up," a program is required to give credit to the many people who have had a hand in its creation. The fact that this curriculum demands cooperative work, however, does not mean that students walk in the door willing to work with strangers or with people they resent, avoid or fear. To help classes work, teachers have to coach students on ways to be productive members of an ensemble. The poster I use to help teach this concept looks like this:

*If You Are a Good Ensemble Member You Can . . .*
- Take Risks
- Ask for and Accept Help
- Bring Out the Best in Others
- Do Your Share by Working Hard and Being Reliable
- Resolve Conflicts Constructively

Adolescence is a contradictory time featuring a great centering on the self while emphasizing an extreme regard for the peer group. Teaching productive ensemble membership builds off this paradox. What we urge students to seek amounts to healthy interdependence, in which they define themselves equally by the group of which they are a part and by their own individual strengths. Ensemble membership is a balancing act, a constant weighing of the needs of the self against those of the group. In building an ensemble, students come to confront the issues of building an active network of learners: that a group is most productive when each member contributes to the fullest extent of his or her abilities, and at the same time, that the sum total of a productive group exceeds its individual parts.

*Ensemble is balancing act (self/group)* · *sum bigger than parts*

Rather than seek a utopian ensemble in which all conflicts are squelched or avoided, students learn to be ensemble members who accept conflict as a natural part of working together. Individuals find themselves forced to make hard choices between supporting the group and standing up for personal beliefs. While theatre's purpose is not to resolve conflict, ensemble theatre shares much in common with the formalized process of conflict resolution. Conflict resolution and management programs in schools, often run by students for students, operate on the premise that conflict is both the obstacle and the step up over the obstacle; that conflict is at once the thing separating people and the thing drawing them together. *Ensemble through risk*

Though risk can increase initial conflict, it is through taking healthy risks that students forge a strong ensemble. This educational philosophy follows the lead of groups such as Outward Bound and ropes courses, which issue challenges to participants that risk their very survival. Though not threatening to their physical safety, standing on stage in front of an audience is a substantial risk to the adolescent's sense of self. Risk defines adolescence, for in risk students test definitions of self and realities of consequence. Ensemble theatre builds off this natural tendency by coaching teens to take constructive risks, as individuals witnessed by others and as a fully contributing member of a group.

Because evaluation scales can teeter between dual abilities, they make apt tools for assessing this kind of learning.

A Student Is a Good Ensemble Member When a Balance Is Struck Between

| | | |
|---|---|---|
| Volunteering to Participate | ←——→ | Encouraging others to participate |
| Having the confidence to take risks | ←——→ | Trusting others to help in risky situations |
| Performing confidently for others | ←——→ | Learning from others as they perform |

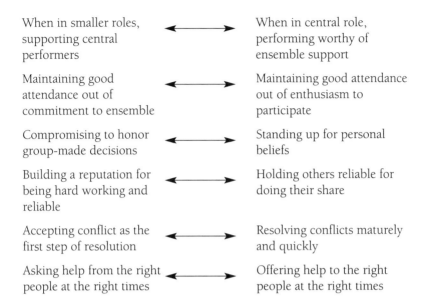

| | | |
|---|---|---|
| When in smaller roles, supporting central performers | ←——→ | When in central role, performing worthy of ensemble support |
| Maintaining good attendance out of commitment to ensemble | ←——→ | Maintaining good attendance out of enthusiasm to participate |
| Compromising to honor group-made decisions | ←——→ | Standing up for personal beliefs |
| Building a reputation for being hard working and reliable | ←——→ | Holding others reliable for doing their share |
| Accepting conflict as the first step of resolution | ←——→ | Resolving conflicts maturely and quickly |
| Asking help from the right people at the right times | ←——→ | Offering help to the right people at the right times |

The tenets of ensemble detailed here suggest a strong similarity with "group work." Collaborative and ensemble work do share a great deal in common, and yet, as the mushroom incident illustrates, they have not in my classroom experience led to the same desired results. One year after beginning my research with Jan, my school district asked me to document educational goals for myself. My number one goal: "To bring the principles of ensemble theatre more clearly into my English classes."

It was the collaborative assumption of the assignment that prompted Megan's unacceptable outburst, and that has raised complaints in other English classes as well:

> Why should students have to share grades?
> Why should a student who sloughs off end up getting free credit?
> Why should a hard-working student get punished for slacking group members?

I usually answer these questions by pointing out that the majority of each student's class grade is based on individual work and that real life expects people to work with one another. My first answer diminishes the

> *Our acting class isn't made up of one person who pulled us all together. I would describe our class like a puzzle; we're just not the same without each one of us. Maybe on a day-to-day basis, people don't realize how important each of us is, but if we're all there, everyone does a better job.*
>
> *Sarah, beginning acting student*

importance of the collaborative work, and my second answer—"You'll need it when you grow up"—does not go far with teenagers.

My attempts to incorporate ensemble work into my English classroom have led to two resolutions: Spend more time on it and gear it more toward performance. In the ensemble drama classroom, work with others occurs daily. While I knew I would be doing group work with my English students, a student would have been hard-pressed to know this by walking into my classroom or looking at the handouts I distribute.

I have made ensemble work in my English classes less of a novelty by describing it, publicizing written information about it, and including it as a category in my grading system. Now the group work done in my English classes is most likely to culminate in a performance. Rather than handing in only a written text at the end of a group activity, students will need to stand up and somehow present what they have learned using multiple modes of expression.

In an exercise designed to introduce the literary concept of foreshadowing, I pass out cards (face down) containing statements such as

> Ms. Wolf will lose her job.
> Ms. Wolf will fall in love.
> Ms. Wolf will win a lot of money.
> Ms. Wolf's house will burn down.

Students are then handed an instruction sheet telling them that, as a group, they must devise and *perform* the following in order to foreshadow what their card says will happen to me:

| | |
|---|---|
| an animal | a sound |
| a body position | a symbol |
| a color | a facial expression |
| a song | |

The students must still write down all of their plans and keep notes of the decisions they make and their reasoning for making them, but when all of the preparation time is used up, they must stand up and perform their foreshadowing choices. Knowledge of this request alone has done more to communicate to students that they must work together responsibly than anything else I have done. The grade is still shared, but complaints diminish rapidly as students realize that each person's individual efforts will be on display along with their abilities to work together. In addition, after one period of acting out these figurative predictions, students are clear on the notion of foreshadowing for the rest of the semester: They can identify instances of it in literature and use it in their own writing.

This was an important outcome for me to observe, because I am not willing to incorporate ensemble work into a nondrama classroom just for the sake of doing it. In this case, the time spent introducing the concept of ensemble is paid back in full by the effective, one-time introduction of the literary concept. Healthy interdependence is fostered, because after the one-day group presentations are over, students are held individually accountable for knowing and using the concept. They will share the grade for the presentation with others, but earn their own grades on exams and papers making use of the concept.

*Interdependence fostered*

## Teaching Ensemble

The exercises in this chapter are consistent favorites with students; these are the ones that they ask for on free choice days, write about in their journals, and tell stories about at home. Were we to introduce them to students as methods for forcing them to share, they probably would not garner such popularity, and yet this is exactly the intent. Students, like all of us, like to get along with the people around them, but they do not necessarily like the idea of having to work with strangers for the first time. Many of the exercises included here are variations on well-known childhood and party games such as tag, musical chairs, and charades—games that have long succeeded at bringing people together into a group and making the process fun. *★ Shared fun*

Shared fun is part of the foundation to building an ensemble, but it is a difficult word to use in education, as it is often associated with undertaught classes or slacking teachers. It is our firm belief that fun and play (in the nontheatre sense) are essential parts of learning; not only do we want our students to have fun in our drama classes, we also want students to see learning on a lifelong basis as fun and satisfying. But as important as it is, fun is not our ultimate goal in teaching the performing arts. To avoid falling into the "game teacher" trap we turn the elements of the ensemble-defining poster and evaluative scales into evaluative questions for ourselves:

Do the students work with a wider variety of ensemble members with each exercise?

Do students take progressively bigger risks with each exercise?

Is a single "star" emerging from the process—a class clown or other talented attention-getter?

Do different students shine in different exercises?
Are students following directions and teacher coachings?
Are exercises starting out serious but dissolving into silliness?
Are we playing games with students or are we taking the time to reinvent games into exercises that teach specific skills?
Are students coming to class to escape from working or to work and have fun?

In her classroom, Jan is expert at keeping planning time short, short, short and moving exercises quickly. Students are always given less time than they think they need to come up with ideas. Protests from students—"No way are we ready!" "We don't even know what we're doing yet!" "That hasn't been as much time as you said!"—She hears as, "We're sitting around getting nervous thinking about all the ways we could fail." To get past this risk aversion, Jan uses lights and music to signal that it is performance time *now*. If students are still getting nervous waiting for their turns in the circle, Jan switches from progressive to random. If a student blanks, Jan keeps right on going with the comment, "We'll come back to you." The pace of the ensemble does not slow for one member, but neither does that member drop by the wayside for the sake of the ensemble.

These exercises take the time to teach something not often addressed directly: how to help one another. Teachers as a group certainly make clear that they expect students to be helpful, and punish students for not being helpful, but we do not always take the time to explicitly teach helping. And yet, as teachers we know that it takes us years to learn how to best help our students.

## Observing the Ensemble

One unique way that Jan takes on the challenge of teaching ensemble is by having her advanced acting class run Central Touring Theater, a drama company that creates and tours an original play throughout the community each year. As an ensemble theatre company, Central Touring Theater draws from a single, known pool of actors to cast its play with equal-sized roles. Most of the students are on stage for most of the play, and there are no stars and no walk-ons. Under the Cast section of their playbill, Central Touring Theater lists each of its members alphabetically, with no designation of who plays which character, since each student is expected to play more than one role during the course of the play. The plays are created patchwork by the entire ensemble, with some scenes memorized from improvisations done in class, some written by individuals, and some composed with the guidance of guest artists. Students may play themselves, fictional characters, or other students in the class—or, most likely, all three.

The actors of Central Touring Theater work within a structure that demands a fluid, flexible group dynamic far away from the carefully prescribed roles—timekeeper, recorder, facilitator—delineated in collaborative learning theory. In addition to the many roles Central Touring Theater members play on stage, they also book their own engagements, design and build their own sets, and set up and take down their show while on the road.

The year I first began observing in Jan's classroom, her advanced acting class was creating a play they titled, "I Shall Not Be Moved." Much of the play is serious, but the ensemble was careful to punctuate the performance with moments of humor. One scene, "You the Man," provided me and the cast with a multidimensional education in ensemble theatre.

Although very short, the scene (about three boys trying to be cool and not show emotion) was popular with the class from the first and continued to provoke laughs throughout rehearsals. It was memorized from the improvisation process and was not scripted until after the play had been performed. I was surprised to see that when it came time to work on it, Jan pulled any three boys at random to rehearse the scene. Usually at least one of the three boys rehearsing would be one of the original improvisers, but in ten rehearsals, I never once saw the scene rehearsed by the same boys twice in a row.

Having created plays with Jan before, students knew that the parts of the scene would be decided upon by the time of performance. While there was a competitive edge to these rehearsals, there was also a strong demand that students "learn from others as they perform." Without a written script, the only way to learn the lines and blocking for a scene was through careful observation. The boys in the ensemble knew if they wanted a shot at a rehearsal audition they had to be ready to participate whenever Jan called on them; no one would feed them lines or walk them through the scene.

> In acting, you've got to be in touch with who you are. You can't be a good actor and not understand who you are and why you are the way you are. You've got to do some soul searching. In every character you study, you are actually trying to find a seed in yourself.
>
> Erica, Central Touring Theater graduate

The scene changed with each rehearsal. If a joke added by improvisation was received favorably by the ensemble, it would appear in the next rehearsal, even if the originating actor was no longer present. The same was true for sight gags, facial expressions, sound effects, and timing issues. In this way, the show became the main focus and the ensemble members its agents. Students were finally assigned to these three roles for the play performance, but because of the shared development process, none of them starred in the scene or owned the piece.

## Using Ensemble

The concepts that Jan and I were investigating as a means of teaching our students were relevant in our relationship as collaborating teachers as well. Any class where the students know one another well and routinely work together to accomplish common goals is an ensemble, which means that any observer poses a problem. Jan and I had agreed early on that when I came to visit her classes in session, I would spend most of my time sitting quietly off to the side and taking handwritten notes on a standard-sized notebook. I would try to observe as much of what was going on as possible and write shorthand notes about it, which I would transcribe each night onto the computer in more complete form.

I showed my notes to Jan (or read to her from them) frequently, and if students asked, I showed my notes to them as well. When class was not in session (and sometimes when it was), I helped out with errands or chores that needed to be done. After and inbetween school hours Jan helped me arrange interview schedules with student and adult members of the Central Touring Theater community, interviews that I taped and transcribed. From time to time I guest-directed a scene or worked with a small group of students to help with a specific assignment. If a class was short one person for a partner exercise, I filled in. I was fairly quiet and serious, at least compared to my personality as a teacher in my own classroom.

Of course, no matter how quiet or cooperative I was, my presence still had an impact, and it was hard for the students to know how to define me in terms of their ensemble. Unlike many other classes I could have been observing, Jan's classes revealed plenty of emotion, personal information, and conflict. As an ensemble, the students held a tacit agreement to take these kinds of risks together and not exploit them, but they could not be sure of my commitment to this agreement, especially since I was sitting there writing down much of what they said and did.

## FIELD NOTE EXCERPT: JAN'S CLASS

### Trust Fall

As I walked into the old choir classroom converted into a theatre, I saw an alarming sight. Two large theatre boxes (plywood cubes painted black, 3'x3'x3') were stacked on top of one another on the lowest-level cement riser built into the floor. On top of the stack of cubes stood a beginning acting student with her heels touching the edge of the cube. Behind her and on the floor stood the rest of the class in two lines, facing one another, and grasping one another's arms. It was clear that the intention was for the girl on the boxes to fall blindly backwards onto the bed of arms five feet below her.

Always more intimidated by the rules and regulations of school life than Jan, I immediately begin imagining all of the things that could go wrong—paralysis, law suits, the principal walking in at any moment. Jan did not even appear to be on the scene. Instead, Levi, an advanced acting student, was guiding the beginning acting class through the exercise. He stood on the second built-in riser, facing the girl on the black box and holding her ankles so that they were lined up against the edge of the box, but so that she did not fall—yet. He was coaching the class by yelling a series of questions:

"Catchers, are you holding one another's arms?"
"YES."
"Are you holding tight?"
"YES."
"Catchers, are you ready?"
"YES."
"I said, Catchers, are you ready?"
"YES!!"
"Faller, are you ready?"
"YES!" (This answer was sort of a scream.)

He then issued a few last-minute safety reminders to the girl: Keep the body tight, fall straight, don't bend, keep both heels right on the box's edge. Then he started everyone off with the call: "Let's count." Everyone responded: "One . . . Two . . . Three." On the count of three Levi let go of the girl's ankles and she fell backward onto her classmates' arms, screaming and then laughing. Once her feet were back on the floor everyone applauded and cheered.

Levi called out another student's name and the whole process started over again. Just watching, my heart was racing, but Jan was off to the side of the room at her desk taking care of some paperwork for an upcoming field trip. She looked up once in a while and cheered after each fall, but was

*I sometimes have the problem that in the junior highs, they don't schedule students of color into my drama classes. So I need to go into the cafeterias and into the study halls. I go in with some of my students and we ask, "Who can we get to come to acting class?" In most schools theatre class typically attracts one kind of kid. The diversity of this program is what makes it what it is. And I just have to keep it that way.*

otherwise not involved. As I furiously took notes and tried to make sense of this whole situation, I noticed Levi looking around the room: "Jennifer!" he called out in his ringleader voice.

Eyes turned in my direction. Jan had made it clear before the activity began that no one was required to fall, but no one refused when Levi called out a name. Refusal on my part would reveal that I was unwilling to do the two things that Jan tells them almost daily are key to forming a strong ensemble: trying and taking a risk. Levi was delighted with his choice to put me on the spot; his smile was direct and challenging. The rest of the beginning acting students were curious to see what an adult would do, too, plus they were keyed up with the heady confidence of having survived the challenge. Jan looked up casually to see what I would do.

I put down my notebook, hiked up my ankle-length skirt, and walked to the box without letting myself stop to think. Once I stood up there with the backs of my heels barely hanging over the edge, I was no longer an outsider taking notes: I was an ensemble member and I liked the support I received. They yelled out their answers to Levi's questions loud and in unison, but even so I had to look down behind me and in a teacherly voice ask, "Now, are you really holding tightly?" "YES!!!" they yelled back.

I didn't like being up there, but I certainly couldn't get down now. I careened backward onto a lumpy stretcher of elbows and wrists and forearms, only to be catapulted right back onto my feet. Everyone cheered. Their challenge was also an invitation.

# Ensemble Warm-ups

*Warm-ups for Cooperation*

## TAPE BALL TOSS

Create a ball by wadding up newspaper and covering it with masking tape. Have students gather in circles of ten and give each group a ball. The objective is to hit the ball in the air and, by taking turns, keep it up off the floor as long as possible. Have the group count the number of times the ball gets hit before it hits the floor. This makes the activity a vocal as well as physical warm-up.

## TUG OF WAR

Divide the class into teams to play a game of tug of war with an imaginary rope. Assign actors specific characters and settings, such as a tug of war at

>  a junior high graduation party
>  a retirement community
>  a faculty picnic

Keep focus on give-and-take to make the rope look real and the game appear believable.

## TUG OF PEACE

With students in partners or in small groups, have students play a game of tug of war with an imaginary rope; however, the focus now is to give and take the rope so there is no winner.

## FAINT BY NUMBERS

The entire group counts off until everyone has a different number. Next have participants mill around closely together in the center of the room. Everyone should be close; however, they should keep moving and try to make eye contact with everyone. Call out one of the numbers, and the person with that number "faints" by collapsing her body, and the group must catch her before she falls. Then instruct the group to walk around again. Continue to call off numbers one or two at a time, and coach the group to maintain a heightened focus to keep the ensemble safe.

## CONDUCTOR

Have students stand in a circle. Divide the circle into four small groups. Suggest an environment such as a school, a beach, or a library and direct each small group to create a sentence that might be said in that place. As a group, their task is first to memorize the sentence so they can recite it together. Next, they are to layer on vocal qualities and movement. Give students a few minutes to practice the presentation of their line. Each group performs their sentence once, then selects a conductor who will stand in the center and conduct the lines. The conductor orchestrates the sentences with hand signals indicating stop or go, loud or soft, fast or slow. This creates an ensemble sound collage of the environment. Try another round where groups use only sound and movement to communicate.

## POWER CLAP

The group stands in a circle and passes a "clap" around the circle. This is done by having two people next to each other clap their hands at the same time; then, moving clockwise, the "clap" moves around the entire circle. Once a smooth rhythm is established, let students who receive the "clap" reverse its direction spontaneously to heighten focus.

### *Warm-ups for Physicalization*

## ENSEMBLE SOLO ONE-TWO-THREE

Working in groups of three, each group numbers off 1-2-3 and then creates its own individual, repeatable movement. Put on some upbeat music and have groups practice their individual movements to music. Use the following commands to lead the activity.

> Number 1: Everyone copies the movement of Person 1.
> Number 2: Everyone switches to the movement of Person 2.
> Number 3: Everyone switches to the movement of Person 3.
> Solo: All participants switch to their own individual movements.
> Ensemble: The three people in each group work together to spontaneously create a movement that include aspects of each individual's movement.

Alternate the commands and conclude with a discussion about the relationship of the individual to the ensemble.

## SOUND AND MOVEMENT CIRCLE

Students stand in a circle. Ask everyone to simultaneously create a three-second sound and movement piece about how they feel. First, have them perform the pieces all at the same time. Next, going around the circle, have each student present his or her own sound and movement phrase. The entire class repeats it back immediately, like an echo. Repeat the exercise, letting students invent their own sounds and movements based on a feeling or a theme of their choice, or have a volunteer stand in the center of the circle and create a series of sounds and movements as the class follows along.

## BUILDING A MOVEMENT PHRASE

Start class in a circle with upbeat music playing. One volunteer stands in the center of the circle and creates a repeatable movement, and the class repeats it. The first volunteer returns to the circle and the next in line moves to the center, repeating the first move and adding on a new move. Take turns adding movements for as long as students can recall the movement phrase, then start over.

## SNOWBALL REVISITED

Students partner up and dance to slow or fast music. When the teacher yells "Snowball," partners break and find a new partner. Coach students to find ways to include and involve everyone. Layer on characters or environments.

## WORDS AND IMAGES

Divide students into small groups. Give each group an emotion; for example, jealousy. Ask each group to decide on five words embodied within jealousy, such as hate, admiration, envy, love, insecurity. Students must create a still image or sculpture for each word for which everyone is involved at all times. Finally, have them connect the images, moving smoothly from one to the next, stating the word or feeling to be revealed before that sculpture appears. Groups practice simultaneously; however, everyone shares their pieces at the end of the exercise.

*Warm-ups for Concentration*

## NAME TEN

Have students sit in a circle and quickly pass around an object such as a key or a hat. Randomly call out, "Stop." Whoever has the object is IT and must name ten things in a selected category, such as

> objects that start with the letter s
> countries
> music groups
> ice cream flavors

IT must identify the ten things while the object is being passed around the circle and must finish before the object returns.

## ENSEMBLE RHYTHM CLAP

Have a volunteer begin by keeping an eight-count beat on a drum. Within that beat, each student, one at a time, creates a rhythm using hands, feet, or both; then the rest of the class repeats it. The focus of this exercise is both on the person clapping the rhythm to create a clear repeatable pattern and on the class listening carefully and repeating back the rhythm pattern as accurately as possible.

## ECHO CIRCLE

This is a fast-paced activity in which changing sounds and movements are passed around the circle. The first person creates a sound and a movement; the person next to her recreates the exact sound and movement and passes it on to the third. The sound and movement jets rapidly around the circle and returns to the originator, where it stops, and the person next in line creates a new sound and motion that is passed around the circle. The game ends when each player has taken a turn to create a sound and movement and the group has passed it around the circle.

## COUNT TO TWENTY

Working in groups of about ten, have students sit on the floor and close their eyes. The object is to have the group count to twenty, with only one individual at a time saying a number. If two people say a number at the same time the whole group begins again with one. The game continues until the group has counted to twenty.

## COMPASS MIRRORS

Students stand in groups of four in large squares. Each member chooses one of the directions on a compass. All students face "North." The student who is North begins to move in slow motion and the other three follow. If person North turns to the East, all follow and East becomes the leader. If East turns halfway around, West begins to lead, and so on. Coach for slow, sustained movement and smooth transitions between leaders.

### *Warm-ups for Sensory Awareness*

## THE PREDATOR AND THE PREY

Students form a circle and two volunteers stand in the middle. One is the "Predator" and the other is the "Prey." The objective is for the Predator to catch the Prey; however, both must have their eyes closed (or blindfolded) and remain inside the circle. Those who form the circle quietly slap their thighs when either approaches the circle's edge. As the

*The Predator and the Prey*

Predator goes after the Prey and the Prey tries to escape, both are forced to use senses other than sight. When the Prey is caught, take two new volunteers.

## NAME SIGNS IN SILENCE

Everyone sits in a circle. Each student demonstrates a hand sign that will be his or her name sign for the game. For example:

head tapping       a peace sign       opening and closing a fist

Establish a group rhythm by having each person slap thighs first, clap hands next, and make the individual sign last. Repeat the rhythm by slapping thighs, clapping hands, and making someone else's sign. When the rhythm is smooth, have one volunteer start using the rhythm and his or her sign, then the rhythm and someone else's sign. The person whose sign was made begins the process again. The exercise proceeds with no talking.

## IMPULSE START AND STOP

Groups of three sit on the floor in a circle and place their hands in the center. On impulse they all begin moving their hands randomly and spontaneously through space. Coach for freedom of movement of hands, fingers, and wrists. Explain that the object is to attempt to stop all hands at the same time, pause for a few seconds, and then start moving them again at the same time. Once students feel comfortable with the exercise, have them stand up and try the same thing moving their bodies. Coach for eye contact. For more challenge, ask the entire class to walk around the room and try the stop on an impulse. Remind students that there can be no leaders; rather, the group should determine its own communication and rhythm.

*When you build an ensemble you have to build it from the first person who decides they want to go into the warm-up circle, energetic and ready to go, to the person who is sitting over there saying, "I'm not getting in any fucking circle." You've got that whole gamut.*

## Exercises for Teaching the Ensemble

### SUPPORT SHAPES

#### Description
This exercise is designed to build support within a learning community. Supporting one another's bodies becomes a metaphor for supporting one another as an ensemble.

#### Considerations
Be aware that this exercise involves low-risk touch. Some students need special coaching through its physical aspects. Music will help to focus the exercise on movement and to keep students concentrating.

#### Procedure
1. Have students find partners of similar height and select a Person A and a Person B.
2. Direct them to create three support shapes using their bodies.

   Support Shape 1: Person A supports Person B.
   Support Shape 2: Person B supports Person A.
   Support Shape 3: A and B depend on one another equally.

3. Once students have created these three shapes, coach them to create transitions that allow them to move from one shape to the next slowly and gracefully.

   Maintain eye contact.
   Communicate your support to each other silently.

4. Give students five minutes to rehearse and polish their support shape performances.

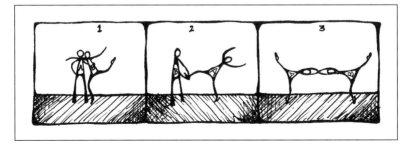

*Support Shapes*

5.  Direct students to sit quietly in a circle with their partner where they will share. Coach for a safe performance space.

    You will all be performing your support shapes for one another. Do not talk during the performance.
    As people take risks you'll see bodies moving in different ways. Be a respectful audience.
    Hold your applause until everyone is finished.

6.  Tap one pair of students at a time to signal their entrance into the center of the circle to perform. As one pair finishes, tap the next pair in to keep the energy flowing.
7.  Follow up with evaluative questions.

    How did it feel to perform?
    How easy was it to depend on your partner? To support your partner?
    Which pairs took risks or made strong connections?
    What did this teach you about working in an ensemble?

    *Variations: Change Theme, Change Group Size, Add Writing*
    Change the focus word from support to another word or concept. Change the music selection. Work in groups of three or five rather than two. Follow with a writing assignment. Perform sculptures while students share their writing.

## SHARING SELVES

### Description
In this small-group activity, students interview each other and create a theatre piece based on the information revealed.

### Procedure
1.  Divide students into groups of three to five. Emphasize the importance of telling personal stories and using our lives as a resource for creation.
2.  Ask students to talk about themselves to the group, one at a time. Provide prompts that encourages them to reveal stories or information that is heartfelt and honest. Members of each group can add additional questions.

    What do you value? What is important to you?
    What makes you mad? What do you fear?
    What do you do to have fun? What pressures do you face right now?

What will you teach your children?
What do you do best?
Who is the most important person in your life and why?

*Another tactic is to let the kid sit there for that day. And we all have a really good time and he watches and sees. And the next day he just comes in; you didn't have to say a word.*

3. Allow ten to fifteen minutes to share stories.

4. From the information gathered, have students create a theatrical piece with a beginning, middle, and end that gives focus to each individual. Encourage each group to get up on their feet and collectively craft a piece that presents the essence of each individual, his or her energy, personality, values, and stories.

   Avoid detailed planning and long discussions.
   Show ideas rather than explaining them.
   Use movement, sound, and images as well as words.
   Involve the entire group in presenting each individual.
   Commit to the transitions.
   Create a strong ending.

5. Each group presents their piece in a central performing area. Follow performances with a critique and feedback session.

   What was being communicated?
   What moments affected you most and why?
   Who took a risk or made a creative choice?
   Which groups maintained strong connections with others?
   What would you change or improve?

6. Broaden the discussion to writers, comedians, poets, actors, and artists who use their lives and their histories as inspiration for their work.

## STORYTELLING IN PARTNERS

### Description

Working in partners, students share personal stories. Then students sculpt images inspired by the stories told.

### Considerations

Recall and storytelling experiences usually go deeper and get more focused when students are led through a short relaxation prior to the activity.

## Procedure

1. Students choose partners and find quiet places to talk and listen.
2. Suggest a focus topic universal enough to assure that everyone will have something to share. Sample topics:

   an extraordinary day in your life
   a time you were treated unfairly
   a difficult choice

3. Instruct students to tell stories to each other. It is helpful to ask them all to keep their eyes closed so they can stay focused and concentrate on using their senses and creating strong visual images.
4. Once the stories have been told, have students come together to sculpt images inspired by the stories. Students sculpt physical images of their stories using the bodies of their classmates. The focus is a sharing of images, that is, stories in a physicalized form. Coach with questions.

   How did you feel talking and listening with your partner?
   Did denying sight make any changes?
   How do you feel looking at the images before us?
   What do you think the story or feeling is for each image?

5. It is not necessary for students to reveal the actual story to the class. You might ask which students wish to share their stories. Also, sharing quietly with one person and building a physical image can be a powerful and inspiring experience. A writing assignment or a discussion focused on the process can provide closure.

## WAKE-UP RITUAL

### Description
This exercise challenges students to recall all events and emotions from a given day and condense them into a three-second sound and movement gesture. Each student shares a gesture and the group repeats it as a way to greet and celebrate each individual in the class.

### Considerations
Music is a helpful pacing agent in this exercise and inspires focus and expression.

### Procedure
1. Ask students to sit or lie down in a comfortable position, close their eyes, and breathe until relaxed. Have them recall their day in detail from the time they woke up to the present moment.

Remember all of the things you have done.
Remember the different feelings you have had.
What made you feel good? What made you feel angry?
Where have you been? Who have you been with?

2. Have students create a starting position representing the moment when they woke up.
3. Instruct students to take four minutes to act out their entire day in silent pantomime. The focus here should not be on recreating every single detail of their day, but, rather, on illustrating through their actions the main events and emotions of their day.

Stay in your own space.
Move very quickly. Don't dwell on any one activity.
Show what happened and how you felt.

4. Now ask students to recreate their days in half the time—just two minutes.

Substitute symbolic gestures and movements for detailed movements.
Keep the sense of a complete day.
Don't lose the emotions that accompanied your day.
Move as quickly as you possibly can.

5. Now drop the time to forty-five seconds and have students recreate their day once again.
6. Finally, have the students reduce their day to three specific, representative gestures, each with its own nonverbal sound.
7. Students rehearse gestures with sounds until they are ready to perform.
8. Students come together in a circle. Pick one student to come to the center, say his name boldly, and perform his three movements and sounds in the center of the circle by himself.
9. Now he leads the rest of the circle in a repeat performance in unison.
10. Continue until each student has performed in the center of the circle.

## CREATING WRITING AND MOVEMENT

### Description
Small groups of students are assigned separate tasks of writing and moving and then combine their work into one theatrical piece.

### Considerations
Two separate work spaces for students are needed, as well as selections of instrumental music if possible.

### Procedure
1. Working in groups of three to six, students designate one person as the Writer; others are the Movers.
2. Gather writers together and ask them to write a creative piece on a given theme:

| | |
|---|---|
| family | competition |
| dreams | neighborhood |

   They are to express how they feel about the topic; however, they are not to identify the topic by name (or by synonym) in their writing.
3. In a different room or space, assign Movers the task of creating a silent movement piece on a different theme. Encourage expression of the theme in the form of sculptures, tableaus, and abstract movement. Require a progression that has a beginning, middle, and end. Examples of themes include.

| | |
|---|---|
| courage | power |
| freedom | fear |

4. After ten to fifteen minutes, coach movers and writers to reunite and combine their separate pieces into one performance.

   Don't worry if the two pieces don't match exactly.
   Trust your impulses.
   Use the music to combine the pieces.
   Writers, read your pieces with feeling.
   Movers, commit yourselves to each move you make.

5. Groups perform their pieces.
6. Be sure to set aside time at the end of this exercise to discuss with students how it felt to combine the two separate pieces. Some find it exhilarating to see the pieces combine; others resent giving up their individuality; others are amazed to see a third piece emerge out of the first two; all gain a deeper insight into what working as an ensemble means.

## SOUNDTRACK

### Description
This small-group exercise focuses on creating a pantomime scene inspired by instrumental music.

### Considerations
This exercise requires recorded music.

### Procedure
1. Students sit in small groups of five. They close their eyes and listen to a soundtrack of selected instrumental music, approximately one minute long. Play the music selection several times.

   ragtime                    percussive jazz
   Gregorian chants           movie soundtracks

2. Students share aloud the images the music evoked as they were listening.
3. Groups have five minutes to prepare improvisations based on these images. Play the music piece throughout the preparation time.

   Everybody up on your feet.
   Use the music to inspire your movements.

4. Groups perform pieces for one another.

   Keep up the pace.
   Exaggerate body and facial expressions.
   Keep the actions connected to the music.

   *Variation 1: Machines or Inanimate Objects*
   Students create a scene with a beginning, middle, and end where actors play the part of a machine or inanimate object. This exercise works best when one group member acts as a person using the machine or object. For example, in a bathroom, students can portray towel racks, towels, shower door, shower faucet. One student can "use" this bathroom by opening the door and drying off with a towel. Other examples include

   a jack-in-the-box          a blender
   a computer                 a piano

   *Variation 2: Costume Pieces*
   Provide students with hats, scarves, pieces of fabric, or simple props to use in their improvisations.
   *Variation 3: Gibberish*
   After creating the improvisation to the music, students add sounds or gibberish to their scene.

## JAMS, CHANTS, AND SONGWRITING

### Description
The following activities teach students to create their own songs. They can be used as isolated exercises or as starting moments for theatrical

pieces. Once the lyrics are established, have students add movement. Survey the class for those who can play musical instruments, collect simple hand instruments, or get creative and use objects in the room to create more complex sounds or rhythms.

## RHYTHM JAM

1. Have students select a theme.
2. Ask for a volunteer to create an upbeat, repeatable rhythm by slapping a desk, beating a drum, or clapping hands.
3. The rest of the group joins in, working in unison.
4. As the group sustains the beat, one at a time students spontaneously take turns creating short verbal verses inspired by the theme. Encourage those who are not yet comfortable with free verse improv to toss in one or two words rather than an entire verse.
5. Try several rounds. If a jam produces lyrics that kids want to save, have them write down their favorite verse.

## CHANTS

1. Have students write a short phrase.
2. Working in small groups, students turn the phrase into a repeatable chant.
3. Next embellish the chant with claps, vocal sounds, volume changes, humming, and so forth.
4. Each small group teaches its chant to the large group.

## SONGS FROM LYRICS

1. Divide the class into groups of two or three.
2. Each group writes lyrics to a song, creating its own structure. The class can work off the same theme or each group can choose a topic.
3. Once the lyrics are finished, each small group shares them with the class.
4. Have students choose which pieces they want to develop into songs and start to work out melody and rhythm.

## TEAM WORDS

### Description

A team activity similar to charades in which the objective is to guess the word being acted out. In this version the focus is on developing acting skills, nonverbal communication, ensemble skills, and spontaneity. This game generates high levels of energy and excitement.

## *Procedure*

1. Students count off into equal-sized teams. Individual teams sit in semicircles with one person—the actor—facing the rest of the team.

2. The following rules distinguish this acting game from charades:

   The actor's task is to act out the assigned word so that team members can correctly identify it.
   The three options for acting out the word are:
   Be the word. (*angry*)
   Deal with the word. (*sandwich*)
   Show the word. (*earthquake*)
   Do not use charade gestures (e.g., sounds like, movie, small word).
   Do not point to an object for identification (such as a shoe or window).
   Do not communicate with teammates by gesture (shaking or nodding head).

3. Each team actor gets the first word from the teacher and returns to her group. Samples include:

   | pizza | earthquake | nightmare | temper |
   |-------|-----------|-----------|--------|
   | diaper | car wash | arrogant | punishment |

4. After each word is guessed, send up the next actor to receive a new word. Rotate team members until each person has a turn as an actor. Keeping score is optional.

   *Variation 1: Partner Acting*
   In place of the single actor, teams send up two actors at a time to receive and act out the word. Partners cannot talk to one another or plan their actions; it is through body language and trusting their impulses that partners discover and define the action in the doing.

   *Variation 2: Continuous Acting*
   The teacher prepares a list of ten words for this fast-paced version in which points are assigned at the completion of a round of ten words successfully guessed. Once the first word is correctly guessed, the next teammate runs up to get word number two. The game continues in this manner until all ten words have been guessed. Try this version in a large space where teams can be spaced far apart and actors have room to run for their words.

*Variation 3: Single Guesser*
Each team picks one person to guess the word; this guesser moves out of earshot while the rest of the team receives a word from the teacher. The guesser immediately returns and stands in front of his or her team. At the command "Go," the team spontaneously creates a group sculpture of the word. The guesser works to guess the team's word. The sculpture remains frozen; it cannot use sound or movement. If the guesser is stuck, the teacher may offer the chance for the team to go into a second spontaneous sculpture, or begin moving in slow motion until the word is guessed.

## CHARACTER CONFERENCES

### Description
This activity begins with physicalizing characters and evolves into a conference or gathering in which all the characters attend and interact.

### Procedure
1. Direct students to move around the room in as many different ways as they possibly can. Give students time to experiment with a variety of character movements.

   Be a character who leads with the hips, nose, or chest.
   Your character is in a hurry; has a headache; is anxious.
   Be a character who has an imaginary string attached to the nose pulling upward.

2. Ask students to select and create specific physical character traits.
3. Instruct students to slowly transform these body movements into real characters; specifically, characters who will be attending an important conference, such as

   a conference discussing juvenile crime in America
   a town meeting on the crisis in public education

4. Inform students that their characters have come to speak and participate at this event. They will be the keynote speakers. Coach them as they walk and establish details of their character.

   You are on your way to a conference about juvenile crime in America. You have been sent to this conference by a particular constituency that expects you to represent them. The choices you make about who you are and who you represent and what your beliefs are should all grow out of the physical position and movements of your character. You may create a character very like yourself in posture and belief, or someone very different. Are you the parent of a child? A police officer? A minister? You are now standing in an empty waiting room in the conference building, re-hearsing your conference speech in your mind. You are passionate about what you believe.

5. Either the teacher or a specially chosen student can act as the moderator of the conference. Cue students that the conference has begun. One by one, students speak at the podium. Encourage passionate and personal speeches.

6. Encourage everyone to speak and respond in character until the moderator closes the conference and concludes the exercise. Repeat with a student-selected topic. For a challenge, try the entire activity in gibberish.

## VOCAL COLLAGING POETRY

### Description
Working in small groups, students create by sharing the text of a poem, a quotation, or a monologue.

### Procedure
1. Generate original writing or bring in selections of poetry or litera-ture filled with images that evoke feelings and explore universal themes.

2. Distribute copies of writing to be staged and allow time for stu-dents to read and react to the material.

   How does it make you feel?
   What is a major theme?
   Where is the climax or strongest moment?

3. Instruct the students to begin by sharing and dividing up the words and phrases in their section. Suggest vocal collaging tech-niques such as:

   speaking as a chorus
   chanting or repeating phrases
   echoing words
   speaking individually or in partners
   varying volume, pace, rhythm
   adding a percussive beat (hand clapping, percussion instruments)
   adding sound

4. Often movement gets mixed into the process of collaging the words. Encourage students to integrate movement and music.

Share your voice.
Listen to each other work together vocally.
Connect emotionally to the piece.
Articulate.
Commit to the feelings of the piece.

5. Have students rehearse and then perform the collaged piece. Remind them to try to stay true to the intent of the piece and make choices that bring life to the meanings or feelings of the work. Direct them to structure it as they would a dramatic piece with a beginning, middle, and end.

## TAG OUT SCENES

### Description
In tag outs, the entire class rotates in and out of the focus scene, changing it with each visit. The inspiration to change scenes comes from the positions of the bodies when the leader calls "Freeze." The focus is on spontaneity rather than mindfully planning a scene.

### Procedure
1. Two volunteers stand before the class. One begins a scene; the other joins in. Actors advance the plot of the scene as well as constantly change the physical picture. The scenes should be dynamic and active.
2. At any point someone can yell "Freeze" to stop the action.
3. Any student can walk up to the frozen scene and tag one of the actors. The tagged actor leaves the scene and the new actor replaces the exact physical position of the first actor.
4. Once in position, the new actor begins a different scene inspired by the frozen pose. This can go on until everyone has had a turn.

## THREE ACTORS AND A BOX

### Description
In this activity students alternately move and freeze and their audience defines scene ideas inspired from their frozen positions.

### Procedure
1. Coach three actors to move randomly around each other and a theatre box.

Keep up your energy.
Keep moving all the time.
Make eye contact.
Take risk.

2. At any point someone can yell "Freeze" to stop the action. Have students in the audience make suggestions for a scene based on the physical positions of the three frozen actors. The situation should be defined quickly and should include character, conflict, and setting. Examples:

   the Statue of Liberty being repaired
   a boxing match with a referee
   two pieces of bread and peanut butter trying to make a sandwich
   two children fighting with their babysitter

3. After defining the situation, the teacher brings the frozen moment back to life and the three actors carry on the improvisation. They must constantly change the stage picture to create new inspiration for the next scene.

4. Change the actors to give others a turn.

*There's fifteen to twenty answers to what I would do with that particular kid. Sometimes I'm very cut and dried: "This is about your grade. If you want to be in this class you need to come over, you need to listen, you need to get in the circle because that's how we start our class. In other classrooms you're in desks. In here you're in a circle."*

## ENSEMBLE TRANSFORMATIONS

### Description
These three acting exercises require students to make rapid changes in emotions, locations, and characters.

## TRANSFORMING LOCATION

### Procedure
1. Select four students and have them stand in the playing area. Give each student an emotion that they are to maintain throughout the exercise.

   excitement      paranoia      jealousy      confusion

2. Select a location.

   bowling alley      toy store      garden      car wash

   On command the four students standing in front of the class begin improvising a scene in the selected location. Their character maintains the given emotion. Every action is driven by that emotion.

Use objects to show how that character feels.
Keep talking; carry on dialogue with other characters.
Talk to yourself as well.
Give and take focus.

3. Keep changing the location. These shifts allow the student to explore many aspects of their emotion in rapidly changing environments.

## TRANSFORMING EMOTION

### *Procedure*

1. Select a Where, a gathering place such as a wedding reception or a baby shower.
2. Select four volunteers. Each volunteer is assigned an emotion.

   pride    anger    excitement    love

3. The first person enters the playing space, motivating all speech and action with the word *proud*.
4. As the second actor enters, motivated by anger, the first actor remains in the scene, but transforms the emotion from proud to anger. Together they improvise angry speech and action at the party.
5. As the third actor enters, motivated by excitement, the first two actors transform from anger to excitement.
6. As the fourth actor enters lovingly, all four actors become loving as they continue to interact and develop the scene.
7. On cue the actors leave the scene in the same order they entered, finding a justification within the scene for their exit. As each character leaves the dominant emotion changes in reverse order until the last person is left and the scene is over.

## TRANSFORMING WHO, WHAT, AND WHERE

### *Procedure*

1. Select five players.
2. The first two players define a Who, What, and Where and begin an improvised scene such as a hairdresser and a customer in a salon arguing over a haircut. Let the scene develop for about a minute.

3. The third player enters and, with words and action, creates an entirely new Who, What, and Where. For example, Person 3 enters as a nurse and sets up a nursing home where she is delivering medication, and Persons 1 and 2 transform into residents.

4. Person 4 enters the scene as an army sergeant and the others transform into recruits at boot camp. Then Person 5 enters as a 911 operator and the others create stations where they place calls.

5. Once all characters are involved, they reverse the sequence. Person 5 exits and the group returns to boot camp. When Person 4 exits, the group transforms into the nursing home. When Person 3 exits, the two in the salon reemerge and conclude their scene.

> *I like using theatre as a device to bring families together and create a community. So, we get together and we have potlucks and I show slides, what we're doing in class, and the kids talk to their parents. Then we get up and do improvs in front of their parents and it really is a nice way for kids who usually don't even get along with their parents to work with them. We've even talked about the possibility of getting parents to do some on-stage theatre work. Sometimes we have parents emcee the performances. I try to make it, as much as possible, a family thing.*

6. Coach for rapid character transitions between scenes, exaggerated character choices, and diverse environments. Add more players to challenge more advanced students.

## TRANSFORMATION SCENES

### Description

This is a great way to generate quick scenes on a chosen topic. Two actors begin a scene; however, the entire class can rotate in and out by tagging out one of the actors and creating new scenes that advance the story line.

### Procedure

1. Two actors begin a scene on a mutually agreed-upon topic. Give this improv forty-five to sixty seconds to develop some depth and interaction.

2. A third person comes quickly into the scene, physically takes the arm of one of the characters, and transforms the moment into a different scene through improvised dialogue and action. The actor not touched sits down and the new scene continues. At any time a new actor may step into the scene, grab one of the actors, and transform the moment again into a new scene.

3. The challenge here is to stay on the theme while exploring as many angles and aspects of it as possible. Coach students to make transitions as quickly as possible and at the highest moment of dramatic interaction.

4. Continue working with student-suggested themes or just remain with one topic and explore it in greater depth. This is an excellent way to bring the entire group into the process of creating moments that could be starting points for more-developed scenes or plays.

# CHAPTER THREE

# Creating

Being social means being creative, creative in how we interact with each other, creative in how we send our messages to each other. We have a responsibility to create for one another.

ANNA CASTILLO

## Defining Creating

In a book about enabling students to turn their own stories into performances, the chapter on Creating is central. Creating depends heavily on the receptive mind and the ensemble and it does not reach its potential without rigorous rehearsal or public performance, but without it, students have not fulfilled their obligations as "social creatures"; they have not "sent their messages." Teachers of the arts are responsible for teaching the process of creation, and students of the arts are responsible for producing creative work, and in this way we begin to fulfill our "responsibility to create for one another." *Responsibility to create for one another*

The creating component is also the central feature distinguishing this method of performance-based education from traditional drama instruction. In this book, creating means coming up with an original vehicle of communication for the theatre. It is demanding and unpredictable. When I asked Jan what was the hardest part of teaching her subject, she answered without pausing, "That part when you're creating with the kids and everyone knows what they want to say but no one has figured out how to say it yet." We both begin the year by telling our students that they will create their own play about something that matters to them and perform it. "Really?" my students respond dubiously. "How?" "That remains to be seen," I answer cryptically. My answer is no act; I do not know the specifics of how their play will come to be created any more than they do. Each class has a different personality, each ensemble has a different message to communicate, and I am still learning how best to teach the creative process.

When I first began this work all I knew was that the traditional plays I was directing (the same plays, not surprisingly, that I had performed in high school) were no match for my urban, immigrant students. Though different from me in most aspects of their lives, my students were like me in that they wanted to "put on a musical"; they wanted to practice after school, work together as a cast, wear costumes, and perform for their families and friends. They ended up rewriting substantial portions of the standard musicals I chose, cleverly and with style, and, watching them recreate shows to fit their lives, I realized I should have had the students write their own piece from the beginning. At first I looked for books about writing original plays with teenagers. When I found none, I began to seek out other teachers writing plays with students.

If I had thought to find a single method of creating original plays with kids, I did not have it in mind for long. Following are some of the approaches I have observed in a wide variety of settings—youth groups, job programs, inner cities, rural towns, counseling programs. Titles are my own, and I refer to youth as students in the philosophical rather than professional sense, as only one of these approaches is actually executed in a classroom setting.

## FIELD NOTE EXCERPT: PLAY CREATION METHODS

### The Tape Recorder Approach

- At this inner-city advanced arts program, the youth group leader spends the first two weeks with a group of ten teenagers sitting around a tape recorder, talking about issues concerning them.
- In addition to talking, the teens engage in warm-up acting exercises and read articles and books related to the topics that come up in their conversations.
- At night, the teacher listens to the tapes of the students' conversations and transcribes them on a computer. In these transcripts he looks for emerging themes and messages. When he finds these, he shares them with the students and uses them to guide further discussion.
- From the discussions and transcripts, the kids decide on the subject for their play.

- Under this topic the teacher writes a skeleton script using the kids' own words from the transcripts.
- The students rehearse, improvise, and debate this skeleton into a final script.
- The company tours their final performance to audiences throughout the city who know their reputation and sign up for their performances in advance.

### The Creative Writing Approach

- In this inner-city jobs program, the group of twelve teens and their advisor have just four weeks to create a one-act play to perform as a touring production.
- The teacher sets aside quiet time each day of their first working week for students to complete open-ended creative writing prompts, such as "Once I saw . . ." or "Mad, mad, it makes me mad . . . ."
- She asks students to read some of their writing aloud and encourages discussion centering around what concerns and commonalities the writing reveals.
- By the end of the week, the students identify themes of common interest to the ensemble.
- The teacher takes home the stack of creative writing papers and over the weekend fashions the strongest excerpts into a poetic script draft under the themes identified.
- She makes sure that each student's writing is included in equal amounts.
- The students read the script draft and decide which lines they want to say and which lines they would rather not say; they add and delete lines as necessary to pull the script together.
- The kids memorize and rehearse the script for performance, which they tour to summer recreation programs for kids throughout the city.

### The Folk Tale Approach

- In this after-school program for immigrant students learning English, the advisor asks students to come prepared to tell stories from their home countries.
- As each person tells his or her story, the others listen and add any details or alternative endings that they may have heard.
- Over a period of about a month, the students tell and discuss stories, analyzing what they have in common and what their deeper meanings are.
- To prepare their performance, students choose a collection of the stories they have heard that fit together under a common theme.
- Their advisor fashions the stories into the first draft of a play, being careful to use a mix of English and native languages.

- At this stage, elders from their ethnic communities are asked to serve as guest directors and comment on the authenticity of the stories.
- The final script contains carefully scripted tellings of the stories, memorized by narrators, as well as planned improvisations acting out the stories' plots.
- Students rehearse both the memorized and improvised portions to prepare for the performance, which can be understood by both English-only speakers and speakers of the native languages included.

## The Scrapbook Approach

- In this small, girls-only college preparation group, the director encourages the girls to collect written artifacts from their own lives: school papers, notes and letters, newspaper articles, poems, report cards, yearbooks.
- Weekly, the girls get together over pizza to share the artifacts they have found.
- As they collect their artifacts, they talk about what they have in common and what is unique. They identify themes communicated by the collection as a whole.
- After about a month, the director fashions excerpts from their artifacts into a choral play draft under the themes identified. Each girl is assigned an equal number of lines.
- The girls debate and rewrite the script draft, switching lines if one decides that she is not comfortable saying something—for example, from her own diary.
- Each girl writes a monologue about a defining moment in her life to end the play.
- The excerpts and monologues are joined into a final script that is memorized, rehearsed, and performed for an audience of family and friends.

## The Improv Approach

- In this urban class, the students are asked to define a pressing problem in their immediate communities.
- The teacher brings to class information about the problem in many different forms: video clips, newspaper articles, guest speakers. She also provides her students with artistic reflections on the problem: poetry, plays, movie clips.
- As the students read and watch and listen, they talk, analyze, and form opinions.
- Once the students have had a chance to consider the issue in depth, the teacher sets up improvisational situations around the problem being discussed.

- When a group improvises a scene with promise, the teacher has them go back over the scene to improve or memorize it, or invites the rest of the class to join in and expand it.
- The teacher offers suggestions in balancing and joining the scenes together into a complete play format.
- Students repeat and rehearse the improvisations until they are memorized.
- Students tour the final performance to neighboring schools and other requesting audiences.

At first observation, these methods reflect the diverse personalities and strengths of the adult instructors: some are trained as teachers, others as youth workers; they are actors, writers, drummers, history majors, anthropologists. But a closer look reveals strong similarities as well.

Similarities:

- Each approach begins with adults asking students to identify what is important to them. And these adults ask respectfully, in ways that make it clear that they intend to listen carefully and learn from the young speakers. When a teenager sees an adult take the time to tape record their words, collect and comment on their writing (without grading or penalizing), or ask to see their scrapbooks, they not only feel important, they take themselves and their own communication more seriously. In turn, they listen to one another in the mature, thoughtful way they see being modeled.
- Each approach makes room for ample discussion with and between adolescents. With the Improvisation Approach, students may spend a whole week talking about one topic, each day exploring a different approach or opinion encouraging discussants to see new points of view and form new opinions. The Folk Tale method has youth discussing their own stories with one another, with the director, and then with community elders. All methods begin with at least two weeks of discussion.
- Each method uses discussion as the basis for immersing teenagers in an area of their own interest. Adults deepen this immersion by bringing in materials that contribute to student interests. In the Tape Recorder Approach, the teacher reads to students from books and articles that address their conversation topics and that they would not likely choose to read on their own. For the Improv Approach, the teacher brings in works of art to complement student concerns in a variety of genres: poems, songs, plays, and essays. With the Scrapbook

Approach, the teacher brings in her own memorabilia to compare with the teens'. Students are immersed on two levels: on a topic of their own interest and on themselves as people with valuable contributions to make.

• All of these approaches also encourage analytical thought. Teens are asked to identify, compare, contrast, prioritize, and predict in the course of their conversations. The Folk Tale Approach asks students to listen to other people's stories with an ear toward what they have heard before and what is new to them. The Improv Approach asks students to look into works of art for opinions and messages about their chosen topic. The Creative Writing Approach asks students to survey their own creative writing for common themes and unique ideas. In this process, students are often asked to consider issues that concern, upset, or mystify them, issues that defy simple solutions.

• All of these methods make room for constructive conflict. In the course of their conversations, teens see that an idea that pleases one person can upset another; that one person's solution is another person's problem. When the adult directors acknowledge the two (or more) sides of an issue, and allow or even encourage debate back and forth, young people are taught to keep their minds open to the possibilities, rather than staunchly backing one idea. Soon students will be taught that conflict is a defining element of drama, and when this happens they will be able to look back on the conflicts they have identified in their own experiences as creative fuel.

• Each of the preceding approaches, while very student centered, depends on the adult being a practicing mentor artist. In each method there comes a time when the adult looks at what the students have generated and fashions parts into a whole. Some adults actually write up a skeleton script; others collage scenes together into an effective order. All tell students what they will do and soon thereafter show them what they have done, always in the form of drafts to be reshaped by the young artists. In the Improv Approach, students improvise off of the teacher's skeletal suggestions. In the Scrapbook Approach, students reassign the lines to various actors and then write their own monologues to complement what has been written. In these methods adult artists model for student artists how to

    reduce repetition
    honor the unique over the cliché
    represent a diversity of voices
    set up a dramatic conflict

• In all of these methods, adults stay close to the teenagers' original words, concerns, and ideas. Young people will perform a professionally-written play that represents someone else's ideas, and they will perform a play that represents their own ideas, but they will not perform a play that misrepresents their own ideas. The Tape Recorder Approach cannot veer far from the students' words, since the script is taken from transcripts. The Creative Writing method, too, fashions scripts directly from students' own words. The act of crafting the draft or backbone of the students' performance piece is a way to model theatre arts, but it is also a test of how well the adults listened to and understood what their students were saying.

• These approaches show students first hand that the act of creating is an act of risk. Each method has a time when the director brings his or her script draft to the students and opens the floor to comments and criticisms. At first teens are given the chance to criticize or reject the teacher's creative efforts and watch how he or she responds. Later they will need to put their own ideas out for critique, as they reshape the script and argue over what points should come first or last, how ideas should be combined, or which language should be used.

• All methods teach students that creating is a process. Creation comes about through discussion, immersion, analysis, and modeling. These methods use no less than seven steps to reach their final performance destination. While steps cannot be skipped, there is no guarantee as to how long each step will take or when a step will need to be revisited. The act of dramatic creating carries with it requirements but follows no formulas; it combines art and logic.

Creating is demanding because it is enigmatic and oppositional. As Jan said, it is the time when people know what they want to say, but not how they want to say it. Students want to believe that their discussions and exercises and time will result in the creation of a play, but it can be difficult for them to maintain the faith when they cannot envision what the result will be. We cannot hang a poster in our classrooms explaining how to create a play, since a play evolves differently with each attempt, but we can and do offer posters defining what we think makes each student an accomplished creator. My creating poster reads as follows:

*You Are an Able Creator When You . . .*
• Surround Yourself with Art
• Actively Pursue Knowledge
• Carefully Observe and Empathize with Others
• Make Original Choices
• Understand/Practice Art as a Process

> *With arts I think kids are given the chance to create the agenda themselves. There's a structure in terms of how to put scenes together, but the issues that are dealt with and the expression that it releases are based on their desires and their fears, not on an agenda that the society has or an agenda that the teacher has. But on their agenda.*
>
> Lacy, intern from Macalester College

These posters help because they put the responsibility on each student to bring to the task of creating an ensemble play individual qualities that facilitate good art and good communication. They also help because they provide an argument to the belief that creativity is a completely mysterious entity, visiting individual students at its own whim—or not. While we know that some individual students have a clear gift for the dramatic arts, we also believe that all students can learn to create and can transfer this ability out of the dramatic realm and into other arenas of interest.

When students practice the tenets outlined on the creating poster, they are preparing for and practicing creation, rather than waiting passively for the creative muse to strike. The Creating Evaluative Scales also make clear that students must practice the skills that lead to creation; indeed, that they will be evaluated on the basis of how consistently they practice these skills. *practice skills to create*

Creating Is a Balance Between

| | |
|---|---|
| Being an audience of live theatre and music performances | Being an audience of good TV, film, and recorded music |
| Reading for enjoyment and information | Writing to record and express ideas |
| Observing people and events with a detached eye for detail | Allowing the self to empathize with others |
| Honestly expressing emotion | Keeping emotions in check |
| Contributing creative ideas to the ensemble | Pulling back to give others a chance to contribute |
| Discerning messages and themes in works of art | Creating original artwork centered around themes |
| Synthesizing ideas | Applying ideas |
| Making original choices | Observing accepted tenets of the performing arts |

Just as the teachers of the play-construction methods bring resources to their students during the creation process, these posters suggest that students bring art and information into their own lives. It is true that this book focuses heavily on having students create their own plays to perform, but this does not mean that we dismiss the large body of published plays in existence. We read and watch these plays with our students, and we assign students to perform scenes from them. We analyze their construction and characters and plots, using them as models for our own projects. *professional plays as models*

The study of professionally written plays is a natural complement to the process of creating original plays; it offers models, choices, and formats. When students critique something I bring in for us to read, I encourage them to create something more to their liking. When students have gone through the process of creating a play with characters, settings, conflicts, and a plot, they are all the more ready to analyze and appreciate these elements in plays written by others. Although Jan and her students are known in their community for writing and performing their own plays, her classes are filled with plays written by others and others who write plays.

Toward the end of each school year Jan also organizes and runs a playwriting festival. For this long-term project, students author their own plays, composing written scripts, as opposed to the methods cited above, and working individually, as opposed to in an ensemble. The goal is for students to create original one-act plays for the festival, and to attain this goal, Jan brings professional playwrights from the community into the classroom to mentor the students. Students entering the festival are required to follow the conventions of playwriting (e.g., listing characters, providing setting descriptions, using dialogue correctly) while creating a unique piece. The finished plays are read and judged by a panel of teachers and mentor artists; the plays deemed most effective and best crafted are produced for performance. *Play-writing festival*

Projects like these encourage research for information as well as appreciation of art. Plays set in other places and times require detailed information to make them believable. Selection of appropriate audition material requires a complete knowledge of the play being auditioned for—its setting, themes, and characters. Use of conflicts requires treatment of a range of opposing opinions. Students who are in the habit of reading for a variety of information have a wider array of topics to choose from each time they are asked to create. All interests are potential inspiration for creation.

The defining and evaluation posters highlight expectations that students become trained observers of the life that is taking place around *students become trained observers* and within them. The students who take the time to see and listen carefully to the events of each day are the students building a creative base of believable details. The students who are aware of their own emotions and who can feel these emotions in others are the students building a creative base of believable characters. Following is a portion of my field notes covering the evolution of an original play by one of Jan's beginning acting classes, a play that requires observation of its participants while making observation its theme as well.

## FIELD NOTE EXCERPT: JAN'S CLASSROOM

### *Creating the Watchers Play*

#### Day 1

Jan sees an editorial in the local paper complaining that the St. Paul community's perception of the students at her high school grows increasingly negative with each new report of adolescent misbehavior. Jan makes a copy of the editorial for each of her beginning acting students and brings it to class on Monday morning.

By the end of the period, the majority of the class is angry with the paper and feels that it "gives in" to negative stereotypes about teenagers rather than taking the time to look at who the students "really are." Jan encourages students to bring evidence of their views to class the next day. As the bell rings, she reminds students that they have a play to create within the month and suggests that if this topic is of real concern to them, they can share it with their family and friends on stage.

#### Day 2

Students look in depth at the evidence they have brought to class. They have some newspaper articles and CD covers plus lots of anecdotal evidence about how the community is afraid of teens. Because Jan has contributed several pieces of supporting evidence to the students' discussion, they are surprised when she turns devil's advocate and shows them a segment from the 20/20 news magazine, with Dan Rather covering one of her past drama classes performing an original play. The video is both professional and very positive about youth; the students in the beginning drama class are impressed and taken aback. Jan casually asks, "What about your play?"

#### Day 3

Jan has students divide into groups of four to improvise scenes showing both overly negative and overly positive stereotypes of teenagers. The students get only ten minutes to create their scenes, and very little in the way of guidelines. They press Jan a little.

"Well, like what do you want?"

"We're going to need all day to do this!"

"You're talking about it too much," Jan interrupts them. "Get up on your feet and do it instead!"

Students scramble to find unoccupied corners of the room and begin acting out their ideas. When they come together to perform, they present the following scenes:

> a satire of the Brady Bunch revealing a sappy-sweet American family
> a reenactment of gang members getting into a fight
> a classroom where students are rude to the teacher and to each other
> a church scene in which the preacher is honoring congregation members for their community work

After performing, the students debrief. "How did it feel to do those scenes?" Jan asks. "How did it feel to watch them?"

"I can't believe we did them so fast!" one students exclaims, and others agree. The students are asked to identify the stereotypes they recognized in the scenes:  *Explore stereotypes*

> All black teenagers are gang members.
> Perfect families have a mother and a father.
> Kids who live in the city don't want to learn.

"It's like people who don't live in the city are from another planet," one girl with a healthy laugh points out, "and they only see a little of what goes on here without knowing the rest of it."

"Let's do a play about aliens from outer space," one young man says.

**Day 4**  *Improv: Aliens on earth*

Jan begins class by referring to the ending of the previous day's class. The students' improvisation exercise for today: Imagine you are aliens watching an event here on earth—positive, negative, or just confusing. Reenacting a scene from yesterday's improvisations is fine. Show how the aliens see what is happening on earth—what they think they understand, what they do not understand, and what puzzles them. The students like this idea and get right to work. New scenes are added to yesterday's collection, including a high school hallway fight and an all-American football game.

For this exercise the students' fascination lies primarily in imagining how others would see them. Postperformance discussion brings out the point that both the football game and the hallway fight might seem the same to aliens: lots of violence, cheering from two distinct sides, some people watching and other people doing. The students are also concerned that their alien observers are only seeing a slice of what happens.

*One of the first things I do in the process of teaching acting skills is sit down and ask, "What's important to you? What do you care about? What things make you angry and what things make you think?"*

"Yeah, the fight looks bad now," a boy in a baggy, forest-green sweatshirt says, "but they probably work it out."

"So what do you want to say to people about this?" Jan asks.

### Day 5

After warming up the students, Jan gathers them in a circle.

"The play festival is coming up. This class is going to do the warm-up performances for the opening of advanced acting's play."

"So, everyone will be watching us?" one student interrupts, surprised.

"How long do we have to stay up there?"

"We don't have enough time."

"We have plenty of time," Jan dismisses. "I've had classes put plays together in a week."

"A WEEK?"

"So, what do you have so far for your play?" Jan redirects.

"Nothing," one girl mumbles with a bit of an attitude.

"I liked your idea about aliens," Jan says.

"Hey! Hey!" one girl shouts out. "We could have aliens come watch us do stuff and, like, show what they think."

"OK," Jan says, looking at a page of notes, "Here's what I need—some volunteers to be aliens." Several hands shoot up. "OK, good. Now everyone else can get into their scene groups from last week."

There is noisy confusion as the students try to sort it all out. In about four minutes they are standing in groups somewhat similar to last week's. Jan directs all of the scenes to run at once, and the aliens to walk among the scenes comparing and debating human behavior.

Before ideas start to run low, Jan thumps on the standing drum and yells, "Freeze!" "This is it," she says in a lowered voice and dramatic tone, "Can you feel it?

The bell rings.

### Days 6–10

Although silly alien improvisations produce laughter from Jan, she does not continue conversation about them the following day. By the end of the week students move toward an idea of wise beings called Watchers coming to Earth to judge. It is decided that the What or conflict of the play will be that the Watchers have been sent to Earth to observe and pass judgment on earthlings, and on Friday the whole class period is spent debating whether they will allow Earth to remain or destroy it. The class seems split, so Jan tables the decision until later, pointing out that it might be easier to make a decision once they know exactly what the earthling scenes are going to reveal.

### Days 11–15

Students run each of the individual scenes over and over as improvs and finally decide on four pairs of opposing scenes:

> a high school hallway fight and a student-run conflict mediation session
> a Brady Bunch family and a dysfunctional family
> a football game and an episode of street violence
> a gang fight and a church service

On most days, these groups go into different areas to rehearse with Jan or an intern and then come back together to perform at the end of class. With each day, students deepen characters and conflicts and memorize lines and blocking. The improvised scenes develop as paired opposites, and when performers are stuck for an idea of what to do, they watch the paired scene and do the opposite. The students assigned to play Watchers fill in for absent students, guest direct, and talk among themselves about what judgments they will pass after each scene.

### Day 16

The class is tense from the moment the bell rings. Posters in the hallways proclaim that they will be performing on Friday night—only four days away—and they still have not decided on the ending for their play. The students bicker and fret, dividing themselves into two camps: pro and anti-Earth. To make things more trying, there are three interruptions—one from a PA announcement, one from a custodian concerned about maintenance of the stage area, and one from the principal, who hopes to have a newspaper photographer stop by later in the day. Two kids goofing off in the corner knock the boombox off the stool where it was perched, creating a distinctly broken sound. It gets quiet. "You don't have to choose between the two endings," Jan says, sounding a little tense.

### Day 17

Jan begins class with a meditative exercise, with the lights low and quiet *meditation* clarinet music playing in the background. "Leave whatever is bothering you today outside the door," Jan coaches in a relaxing voice. "Feel your body relax. Imagine that you are lying on the warm sand of a tropical beach. You have been sent here, all expenses paid, to imagine endings for our play. Everything you need is taken care of; all you have to do is be creative. Whatever you can imagine can become reality on the stage. Push yourself to think of something totally different. What do you see?" Slowly she turns the lights back up and fades the music out. "What did you decide?" she asks.

Today the ideas are flowing. Students blurt out their ideas without bothering with the formality of raising hands, one right after the other. Their final decision is a compromise: The Watchers will hold a hearing after observing all the scenes. They will debate among themselves, using the evidence from the scenes to back up their respective pro and anti-Earth opinions. Finally they will agree to freeze Earth as a museum, so that other beings can come to learn from the good and bad lessons its inhabitants have to offer. This idea starts as a suggestion after the meditation exercise and is completed with some improvisation exercises that elaborate on it. By the time the bell rings, everyone seems pleased with the ending they have found. **Decide on ending**

## Days 18, 19, 20

The class furiously practices their play, at first in segments and then as a whole. Classtimes offer only minimal warm-up activities and diversionary exercises; everyone is eager to iron out the wrinkles, memorize their parts, and "get it right" by Friday night. The questions that arise:

Should the gang members use weapons?
Should the Watchers calmly debate the issues or argue with emotion?
Should the mock Brady family members enter with silly instrumental music?
Or should someone try to tape the actual theme song?

get resolved quickly now. They no longer enjoy the luxury of indecision.

---

The Watchers' scene illustrates creating as a process. It is not a formulaic, predictable process. But it does have a definite beginning, the challenge issued by Jan on Day 1, to create a performance that conveys meaning, and an end, the original performance piece that conveys meaning. We know that the students and teachers who engage in this process will have to endure dissension and disagreement and maybe even a feeling of "This is never going to work." We do not arrange for these feelings of contraction and difficulty, certainly, but we also cannot think of a time when they have not occurred as students create plays.

Postperformance discussions, such as those on Day 4 and Day 6, center on two types of reality: (1) Do their portrayals of other people ring true? and (2) Do their projections of others' opinions ring true? Onto these scenes of life around them the student creators impose a third, metacognitive layer of observations when on Day 10 they create the device of the Watchers coming to observe humans and form opinions. As actors, only a few students perform the parts of the Watchers. But as play creators, each student in the class has to observe, think, and make decisions like a Watcher. Jan's students observe themselves observing themselves.

The difficult moments surely stem in part from teenagers' awareness throughout the process that they will have to stand up in front of others and perform what they create. On Day 6, when Jan formally announces the specifics of their upcoming performance, the students let their fears surface and for the first time we see an attitude in the classroom. Day 16 is the hardest. It is as if the whole idea of creating and performing an original play is so overwhelming that it would be easier to get mired in disagreement and toss the whole thing. But as wearing for Jan as a day like this is, she does not lose her temper nor does she give in. There is nothing in Jan's reactions to which the students can channel their anger, and so they are left to look at themselves and their own behavior.

Jan did not enjoy Day 16, but she knows that the difficulty is a turning point in the creating process, one that is good to have in the rearview mirror because it signals a move toward an end. Like her students, Jan takes on the creative challenge to be an observer. By carefully observing her students and accepting the process of creation as one that moves through stages, she is able to guide the students to a finished, successful performance.

## Teaching Creating

*Exercizes require discipline*

The exercises presented in this chapter both model and require discipline. In addition, they provide direct instruction on the basic tenets of dramatic art. Any subject matter has basic properties, theories, and ground rules students must learn to become fluent in that domain. The dramatic arts are no exception. In a traditional drama class, students study the basic tenets of dramatic construction by analyzing plays written by others. While students in Jan's class do study existing plays, emphasis is on creating original plays, and so these basic tenets are taught through the classroom exercises that Jan has designed and collected. The daily repetition and challenge of these exercises teach students the building blocks of dramatic creation.

The improvisation exercise students engage in during the play creation process demonstrates three of the most basic requirements of any

> *In our play we don't just talk about our ideas, but we talk about ourselves and our lives. You can put yourself back into a painful situation, only it isn't as bad as it was the first time, and it isn't as hard when you have to deal with it again.*
>
> Amara, beginning acting student

dramatic scene: a Who, a Where, and a What. This exercise teaches quickly and effectively that the Who equals character definition; the Where, setting definition; and the What, conflict definition. Students in Jan's class will perform this exercise more than once, and ones like it over and over again. Even within the exercise itself there is ample repetition: Everyone in the class gets a chance to try and also watches as everyone else tries. Because the exercise is structured so that each actor's entrance cue is the display of a satisfactory Who, What, and Where by the previous actors, everyone is diligent in analyzing, and ultimately memorizing, these three elements.

*Analyze Who/What/Where*

Students quickly begin to see these three elements in other kinds of narratives: comic books, music videos, cartoons, or mystery novels. In more advanced exercises, such as those that fall under the category Inspiration for Scene Work, a student's failure to clearly define a character, setting, or conflict results in boring, undefined work.

When Jan instructs beginning students to work on scene construction in groups, I often observe a brief "dead time" where the students look back at her with lost expressions and say things like, "What are we doing?" or "There's no way. . . ." Jan is expert at not giving in to the students' doubts; instead of sympathizing with them, giving them more time, or walking them back through the directions, she repeats key coaching phrases that they have heard before in creating exercises. "Remember Who, What, and Where," she might repeat for the class at large, or, "Take a risk when you choose your Who, What, and Where. Give us something new!" The familiar words and well-studied elements strike chords of recognition for the students, and give them the tools they need to get to work.

Deciding on an appropriate ending poses a challenge to students learning to create. Just as Jan gets better work out of her students when she gives them less time rather than more, she teaches that scenes are better ended by leaving the audience wondering and engaged rather than wishing the show would end. As a tool for creating powerfully ended pieces, Jan teaches the concept of the heightened moment. At first Jan identifies heightened moments for her students as they perform, and then she expects them to be able to choose this moment themselves. In the following transcript, Jan uses the Statue Tag warm-up exercise to teach this lesson.

## FIELD NOTE EXCERPT: JAN'S CLASSROOM

*Statue Tag*   to teach heightened moment

Twenty-two students are frozen around the stage space, posed as famous inventors, until they are tapped to life by Jan; they then improvise a short monologue as their character. Jan has a whole class of sculptures to bring to life, and she wants to give everyone a turn; if twenty-five students speak for one minute each, half of her class time is used up and students have been frozen for a painfully long time.

She listens carefully to each performer for a phrase that is unique, arresting, or problematic, and then stops them immediately. In the monologues recorded here, the double slash marks indicate where Jan refreezes the student to end the monologue.

> OK (*pause for a breath*). I am Cheryl Darnley, and I have invented the cure for cancer. Cancer has been a terrible curse on our world for hundreds of years. I'm not the only person to have suffered from it. When my mother died//

The student speaking stops exactly when Jan signals her to, but looks surprised, as though she was just getting going. A few of the other students momentarily break their freezes to look at Jan, to see why she stopped the student so quickly, or to look at the student to see if she minds. "Hold onto your freeze," Jan coaches. She immediately taps a second student to start his monologue, and the rest of the students regain their concentration. They are getting the message that things will be moving too quickly for them to allow distractions. The tapped student speaks:

> I always hated pollution. Where I grew up the skies were dirty with smog all the time. It made my eyes sting and my throat burn. So I knew I wanted to invent something to clean up our earth//

These two monologues demonstrate the benefits of having students create as an ensemble. Here the students learn from observing others try, but always in the knowledge that they will have to try as well. Immediately students need to reprogram themselves to understand that being stopped by the teacher in this exercise is not a negative assessment, but a sign that they have achieved.

Jan, located in a theatre space far away from other classrooms, uses music every day to relax, motivate, and pace her students. In an exercise such as Song Scenes, students can use music as a creative scaffold, borrowing from the song's lyrics or musical structure to create their

music as creative scaffold

scene. Providing a list of requirements to include in a creating task promotes unique final products. When lost or stuck, students can look to this list of constants to give shape and depth to scenes. For each scene assignment, I write the four or five "required elements" on an easel notepad that I set at the front of the room. Jan is more likely to tell the class the requirements and then reiterate them as she circulates. The following complete list of the required elements collected from all of the exercises in this book reveals the wide array of tools that can be given to students as they learn to create.

*required Elements:*

### Written Texts
published poetry
original poetry
journal entry
lines from other plays
newspapers

### Sounds
recorded music
silence
instrumental music
percussive beat
sound effects

### Speaking Techniques
vocal collage
gibberish
repeated lines
simultaneous speech
foreign languages

choral speech
echoing

### Movement Techniques
slow motion
mirroring
impulse work
resistance moves
pantomime

### Objects
provided props
found props
fabric
illustrated scenery
costumes
symbolic object

### Other
specific emotion(s)
themes

These elements can be inserted into any creating exercise and used in any combination. Simple exercises can require a single element; more challenging exercises can layer several elements into a performance. Elements can also be tailored to a group's strengths and weaknesses. For a group that is verbally shy, for example, beginning by requiring gibberish can be a helpful choice; later, progressive requirements of chants, group speech, and pair speech can ease students to present brief monologues.

Creating is demanding work for both reluctant and enthusiastic students, for teachers and professional artists. The ability to produce original thought, in any realm, receives a different breed of attention than the ability to study someone else's thoughts or copy them. Whether they engage in a short creating warm-up, a project to create an ensemble scene, or the long journey of creating an entire play, students feel pride when they create.

## Using Creating

Jan and I found it fulfilling to work on the long-term project of the book, but our times together rewarded us with more immediately usable material as well. During the summer we worked on the creating chapter, together we sketched out a four-week unit to introduce the creating concept. What follows is the monologue unit plan I adapted from our original outline. For this unit, students write one monologue draft per night for a week, then select, rewrite, edit, and type a final monologue. They also memorize, rehearse, and perform their monologues for a grade.

### CLASSROOM ASSIGNMENT: JENNIFER'S CLASSROOM

*The Monologue Unit*

| | |
|---|---|
| Week I | Getting to Know One Another |
| Week II | Monologue Creation Week |
| Week III | Rewriting Monologues |
| Week IV | Rehearsing and Performing |

*Week II: Monologue Creation Week*

Day 1: Scene Starts in a Circle

- Do Scene Starts in a Circle exercise.
- Have students use the line of dialogue they create in the exercise as a start-up for a quick monologue.
- Make a few suggestions to get writing started. For example:
  Explore all the things going on in the character's mind.
  Write what you would like to say back.
  What would you prefer to be said to you?

Day 2: Talking Furniture

- Have students pick a room in their house—but not a bedroom or a bathroom.

- Have them close their eyes and visualize the room: being in it, remembering its details, what it's used for.
- Have students draw the room using at least twenty details, such as furniture, floor or wall coverings, appliances, and fixtures.
- Have students select one of the most unique details and share it.
- Choose one of the details and create a monologue from its perspective.
- For example, if the sofa had a mind of its own, what would it think?
- Share ideas for monologue starting points.
- Write.

## Day 3: Fill-in-the-Blanks

- Read sentence starters to students such as:
  - Me, myself, and I ———
  - Let me tell you why ———
  - Mad, mad, it makes me mad ———
  - Once I saw ———
  - If I could ———
  - People here ———
  - In my mind I hear ———
  - And one more thing ———
- Encourage students to write honestly and with detail.
- Each student picks one sentence to share.
- Have students select a line (theirs or someone else's).
- Write a monologue using this line as the first line.

## Day 4: Slashwrite

- Play several selections of music.
- Ask students to think about what pictures and emotions the music suggests.
- When they are done listening have each student finish this sentence:
  Listening to this music made me feel ———.
- This is the starter sentence for their monologue.
- In this monologue each sentence will begin with the last word or phrase of the preceding sentence. For example:
  Listening to this music made me feel nostalgic. Nostalgic because it reminds me of my grandma, who used to play the piano before we went out to pick the tomatoes and squash on her farm. Her farm was my favorite place to be when I was a kid. A kid, running from cow to cow as she was milking, hoping for some fresh milk.
- Allow for three or four exceptions to the last word/first word rule for variety.

## Day 5: Bringing Artwork to Life

- Gather a selection of artistic renderings of people.
- Set up the room like a museum.
- Encourage students to wander and look without speaking, and to try to empathize with the people in the pictures.
- Have students physically become a character in one of the pictures, freezing in the same body position, facial expression, and mood.
- Encourage students to try to think like their character as well.
- Once students have returned to their own bodies, have them write an interior monologue exploring what that person in the picture is thinking.

### *Week III: Monologue Rewriting Week*

## Day 1: Understanding the Basics of a Monologue

- Perform a monologue for the class, such as
  *F.O.B.*, by David Henry Hwang
  *Fences*, by August Wilson
  *The Dark at the Top of the Stairs*, by William Inge
- Class analyzes who, where, when, and conflict.
- Repeat the exercise with other scripted monologues.
- Have students again define who, where, and so forth.
- Students go back to their rough drafts and select their favorite.
- Students begin rewriting to include the basic elements discussed.

## Day 2: Going to the Movies

- Repeat the previous day's exercise with monologues on film for example
  Marlon Brando in *A Dry White Season*
  Whoopie Goldberg in *The Color Purple*
  Rosalind Chao in *A Thousand Pieces of Gold*
  Edward James Olmos in *Stand and Deliver*
  Steve Martin in *Roxanne*
- Have students continue to rewrite drafts with basic elements as well as edit for repetition, clichés, mechanical errors, and other flaws.

## Day 3: Theatre Exercise Day

- Choose exercises to hone whatever basic creating skills needs tuning, such as
  Recall
  Hitchhiker
  Basket Scenes
  Trigger Skits
- Take students' monologue drafts home to read and comment.

### Day 4: Read, Share, and Rewrite

- Put rewriting questions on the board, such as:
  Have you used all five of the senses?
  Have you used color?
  Do you use at least three different emotions?
  Does your monologue have a clear beginning, middle, and end?
  Does it have a heightened moment?
  Does it include stage directions?
- Have students read each other's monologues and your comments. They can use questions on the board for structure.
- Distribute Response Sheets for sharing monologues with family members at home.
- Remind students to hand in a final draft the next day, and to print up two copies—one to hand in and one to keep.

### Day 5: Performance Basics

- Use minilecture and participation games to teach such basics as
  entrance and exit
  use of stage space
  projection and enunciation
  comfort on stage
  memorization skills
- Give students time to begin memorizing their monologue scripts.

### Week IV: Rehearsal and Performance

### Day 1: First Rehearsal

- Have everyone stand up and recite their monologues at the same time.
- Ask students to rehearse their monologues without using words.
- Talk about the difficulty of defining body movement, emotion, and gesture.
- Ask students to color-code their scripts for emotions.
- Have them also draw stick-figure representations of their blocking.
- Rehearse for tomorrow's memorization drill.

### Day 2: Memorization Drill

- Give students warm-up time to practice memorization.
- Call students up one at a time to recite memorized monologues.
- Lead class through a volume rehearsal. Have them recite their monologues as they
  whisper          shout

```
laugh          cry
mutter         sigh
```

- Evaluate the exercise and have students apply the critique to their monologue performances.

### Day 3: Orchestrated Rehearsal

- Start with a diagnostic rehearsal. Have students pick their most problematic line.
- Invite students to perform and then take suggestions from the audience.
- Orchestrate a rehearsal of four or five monologues at a time, freezing and unfreezing individual performers until each is done.

### Days 4 and 5: Performance

- Offer brief rehearsal time.
- Lead a meditation or other relaxing focus-builder.
- Lead the class through physical and vocal warm-ups.
- Have students in the audience write letters to each performer after each performance.
- Those who have just performed can write a letter telling how they think they did in their performance.

> *When you're in the process of creating, you're whole and sane and healthy, and somehow, as a human being, together. It's a release from everything else, but it includes everything else. You're able to feel the world, take it in, and then put it out there in a creative form. It's part of what being human is; that's why culture and the arts have lasted.*

## Warm-ups for Creating

### Exercises for Spontaneity

### MACHINES WITH THEMES

Have students create a human "machine." One student begins by performing a simple repetitive sound and movement. The next person joins in by making a connection while initiating her own sound and movement. Students continue to join in to enlarge the machine. For round two, have students select a theme such as war, temptation, or justice. Repeat the exercise with sound and movement inspired by the theme. Allow students to replace the sound with a sentence or group of words. To conclude the exercise, challenge students to stop the machine on impulse all at the same time.

### STATUE TAG

Begin with a standard tag game. IT freezes as soon as she or he tags someone else. The person they tagged becomes the next IT. The game continues until everyone is frozen like statues in a sculpture garden. Direct students to remain frozen and begin creating a character as soon as they assume their statue positions. You can give a character prompt, such as

> You are a statue of an inventor, past or present, real or
> imaginary, who created something to help humanity.

Tap each statue one at a time to bring it to life for a short monologue based on its character.

### CAR PLAY

Arrange four chairs to simulate a car. Have two volunteers sit in the front and one in the back. The fourth person enters as a character and the others in the car take on his or her characteristics as they take a "drive." A new passenger enters and sits in the fourth person's seat as a new character. Students rotate, the driver exits, and everyone in the car takes on the characteristics of the new passenger. Continue the rotation until everyone in the class has had a turn. Encourage characters that are animated, both physically and vocally.

### STORY-ACT

A volunteer tells a story, real or make-believe, written or spontaneously created. As the storyteller describes characters and action slowly in

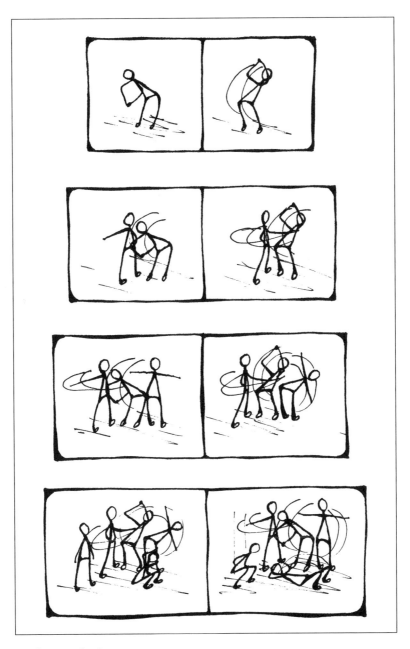

*Machines with Themes*

detail, the student actors physicalize the story silently, in an exaggerated and highly animated style. Coach for a unity between the narrator's description and the actors' actions.

### *Exercises for Concentration*

## LONG CHARACTER MIRRORS

Divide the class into two groups. Have them stand in two lines facing each other and tell them to imagine a long mirror dividing the lines. The mirror cannot be crossed. Assign one group to be characters and the other group to mirror their actions. Set a scenario for the characters such as junior high students backstage practicing for a talent show or chefs in a restaurant preparing food. Provide music that fits the environment and have characters begin a pantomime improvisation in the chosen setting. The group mirroring the activities should work on creating an accurate reflection. The characters should be coached for detail and sustaining a variety of activities. Reverse roles and begin again in a new environment.

## SIMULTANEOUS STORYTELLING IN GROUPS

Start with three volunteers and work up to five. Students stand close together so they can hear each other speaking. One at a time each student begins telling a story beginning with "Once upon a time." Each story at its inception is unique and separate. As all players tell their stories, at

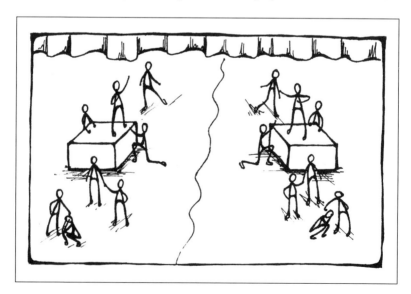

*Long Character Mirrors*

the same time they are carefully listening to others tell their stories. The object of this challenging listening exercise is for the players to begin to integrate words from each other's stories into their own stories, and finally to develop a three-to-five word phrase that evolves from listening. The problem is solved as this phase is repeated in unison over and over again by the players and the teacher stops them on command.

## PREGNANT SILENCES

Working in groups of two or three, have students create a short scene using only pantomime movement and action to establish who, what, and where. There must be an unspoken tension between the characters that is felt and communicated but not spoken. Instruct students not to mouth words or imitate speech. The scene should be at least one minute long. When the first word or sentence is spoken, freeze the scene. Discuss choices with the group.

### Exercises for Writing

## COMMUNICATING STORY AS ACTION

Have students imagine a scene that can communicate plot with action rather than dialogue. Have them write out a detailed narrative for their scene with a beginning, middle, and end. Have students read scenes and take volunteers and bring the scenarios to life.

## SLASHWRITE

Select a topic or have students work with their own ideas. Instruct them to write on the topic for a given amount of time using the following structure: At the end of every few sentences make a slash mark on the paper. This slash means that the next sentence should start with the last few words of the sentence before. For example:

> When my sister was born I held her tiny body in my hands./ I held her tiny body in my hands and felt love for the first time./ For the first time I cared about the future./ The future was in her eyes./ Her eyes . . .

When they are finished have students choose partners and read their pieces to each other, then select one to present together to the class.

## CHARACTERS FROM MUSIC

Begin a short relaxation to enhance focus. Next play a selection of music and ask students to visualize a character inspired by the music. Have them write a quick description of their character, including name, age, and other details that come to mind. Repeat the exercise with two other contrasting selections of music. Ask students to select one character with which to work. Have students stand and begin to create the character physically. Select an environment such as a restaurant or bus stop and have characters enter and interact.

### Exercises for Character Development

## TALKING SUBTEXT

As soon as students walk in the door, hand them a piece of paper with a short sentence or group of words written on it such as, "the sky is blue" or "on the other side of the street." Instruct students to memorize the line. Next, suggest an environment that would facilitate interaction, such as a class reunion, wedding, or convention. Ask students to create a character and interact with others in the group; however, they can only use the words in the sentence to communicate.

## GOOD-BYES

Have students choose partners. Explain that they will create a short, silent moment focused on two characters saying good-bye to each other. Instruct them to define who the two characters are as well as the details of the situation. Have one person leaving and the other staying. Next, have partners sit next to one another on chairs or on the floor. Encourage minimum movement and maximum eye contact. Adjust the length of the exercise to the concentration level of the students. Before students talk about the experience, have each person write a short letter to their partner about how they felt.

## POETRY TO MONOLOGUES

Each student receives a short poem. After reading it they must transform the poem into a monologue by creating character, place, and motivation. Have students take turns performing their pieces. Have the class try to guess details about the character and circumstances.

## INTERNAL MONOLOGUES

Ask one student to create a sculpture of a character in a frozen pose, expressing an emotion. Have classmates observe the body position and facial expression and imagine who the character is and what the character is thinking about. Next have students take turns creating the character's internal monologue by standing next to the frozen character and speaking the character's thoughts. Encourage students to create internal monologues that contrast with the external appearance. For example, an internal monologue can reveal a frozen character, who appears joyful but is actually filled with anxiety.

### Exercises for Scene Work

## NINE-WORD SCENE

Instruct students to get into groups of three. Ask each person to write three words on a sheet of paper, one of which should be his or her name. Each group then has a collection of nine words that will become a script for its scene. Give groups ten minutes to create a theatre piece with a beginning, middle, and end, using only nine written words as their script. They can order the words any way they like, repeat or share the words, and use words for what they mean or as gibberish, but they may not add new words.

## SONG SCENES

Select a track of music with lyrics and a strong theme that could inspire an idea for a scene. Ask students to get into small groups of three to five. Have them listen to the song with their eyes closed and allow images to come alive in their mind. Explain to students that they will have ten minutes to create a scene with dialogue, and the music must be played somewhere in it. They can have the action go with the music, against the music, or satirize it. Before performing, they should give the exact cue line for starting and stopping the song.

## DEAL-A-SCENE

Each student gets three file cards. On the first card instruct students to write a location, such as

> an amusement park
> the top of the mountain
> a library

On the remaining two cards, describe two different characters. Include age, emotion, and character identifiers. For example:

> a forty-two-year-old frustrated hospital worker
> an eighty-one-year-old silly grandparent

*Every play is different. You find the answer in the work. Sometimes the kids are really worried in the beginning about how it's going to end. And it's hard for them to let go of that because usually, we figure out the ending about a week before we're going to open. No matter what it is, all the pieces will line up and show what the ending is.*

Have students line up their character cards face down on one side of the room and their location cards face down on the other side of the room. Have students find a partner. One person gets two character cards while the other person selects one location card. Give students five minutes to create a scene using the information on their cards.

### Inspiration for Scene Work

Included here are structural ideas useful as starting points for extended scene work and ensemble play making. The process of identifying themes for original work is an unpredictable journey unique to each group. Creating together allows an ensemble to explore issues and identify its collective voice. The ultimate challenge for the teacher in this process is to provide leadership so that the voice, perspective, and feeling of the ensemble guide the process and the product.

## BASKET SCENES

Each group is given a basket containing a variety of items such as a tablecloth, a rose, a poem, a taped piece of music, a necklace, and a hat. Students work together to create a theatre piece that is inspired by the objects and uses all of them in the scene.

## GIVEN STRUCTURE: A JOURNEY

Give small groups "a journey" as a structure for an improvisation. For example:

- A young person is in some kind of conflict at school, at home in a relationship, or within themselves.
- The conflict escalates to the point that the young person decides to leave the situation altogether.
- This main character then goes on a short journey and encounters these elements: (a) an object; (b) a supernatural force; and (c) an obstacle they are forced to deal with and overcome.
- At the completion of the journey, the young person returns home and resolves or learns to manage the conflict that originally drove them away.

Have students plan, rehearse, and perform each journey as a short play.

## ENSEMBLE POETRY

Bring in selected poetry or help students create their own individual or collective poems. Let the poem serve as a springboard to creating a theatre piece. Work with students to develop an ensemble presentation of the poem. From there students can create scenes, songs, and monologues and expand on the themes and feelings presented in the poem.

## A PLAY IN A DAY

Have the class agree upon a theme. Next ask students to get into groups by form of expression, such as poetry, monologues, dance, singing, visual art, or storytelling. Each group creates a piece on the topic in their chosen form of expression. When the groups have completed their work, the ensemble joins together to sequence the small pieces into one artistic piece and perform it.

## RANDOM CHARACTERS

Divide students into groups of four. Each group is to create a story focusing on one person as the central character. The story is to take place in the past or in the future. Assign specific but unusual character roles, such as:

Person 1 will be the central character
Person 2 will be an object
Person 3 will be a body part
Person 4 will be a supernatural force

Suggest that the scene focus around the central character. Begin at a heightened moment of dramatic action and end with a resolution or a frozen moment of action that leaves the conflict unresolved.

## DREAM SCENES

In small groups, have students share dreams that they have recorded or remember. Ask them to select one person's dream to stage. A creative method to work with dreams is to avoid language and use images and sound. A framework including beginning, middle, and end; large physical images; and handheld instruments to underscore events or characters can bring the images of dreams to life.

## GENRE SCENES

Generate a list of theatrical genres, such as western, soap opera, melodrama, comedia, horror, adventure, opera, musical, silent movie, or mystery. Have students select a topic and create a piece using one of these styles. Have matching music on hand.

## Exercises for Teaching Creating

### LIVING NEWSPAPERS

#### Description
The following theatre exercises use the newspaper as the source for creative work.

#### Considerations
Have available a selection of newspapers or preselected articles. Note that this is a quick exercise for which setting time limits and sticking to them yields the best results.

#### Procedure
1. Divide students into groups of five. Each group gets an entire newspaper or a group of selected articles.
2. Students have five minutes to select something from the paper on which to base an improvisation.
3. Assign students to improvise a piece in fifteen minutes based on their selection.
4. Give students specific suggestions to help them create and focus.

   Use the headline or actual sentences from the article in your scene.
   Let your piece reflect a specific point of view.
   Create a scene in two parts beginning in silence and ending with dialogue.

5. Each group performs its piece.
   *Variation 1: Character Monologues*
   Each student in the group takes on a real or imagined character inspired by the article and writes a short monologue expressing that person's point of view. The students then decide how to connect the monologues into a single performance piece.
   *Variation 2: Object Monologues*
   Students write monologues from the point of view of an object involved in the article, such as the car involved in a drunk-driving accident, the gun used in an armed robbery, or the hoop in a basketball game.
   *Variation 3: Living Newspaper Performance*
   Expand this exercise into a week-long activity by generating scenes, monologues, or songs inspired by news stories and linking them together. Assign research on topics that require more detail. Use poetry or music for transitions.

## RITUALS

### Description
Working in small groups, students create a ritual ceremony based on a theme that serves to strengthen and unify a community.

### Considerations
This exercise can easily extend to fill three to five hours. Quiet space for groups to use in rehearsal is helpful. Provide each group with a collection of suitable props, such as fabric, musical instruments, nature items, masks, and recorded music.

### Procedure
1. Begin this exercise with a guided question-and-answer discussion about rituals. It's helpful to record students' answers on the board or on butcher paper.

   What is a ritual?
   What kinds of rituals can you think of through history and across cultures?
   What do these rituals celebrate? What purpose do they serve?
   What are some things that all of these rituals have in common?
   Why do you think rituals have lasted across time?
   What rituals are you familiar with from your own culture?

2. Generate a list of possible ritual topics.

   | | |
   |---|---|
   | birth | harvest |
   | death | healing |
   | marriage | coming of age |

3. Gather students in groups of six.
4. Each group's task is to create a unique ritual with a beginning, middle, and end lasting approximately three to five minutes. It should include

   a brief creative written piece (poem, letter, journal entry)
   the ritual activity
   a group sculpture
   use of props or material provided
   no spoken dialogue (humming or chanting is OK)

5. During rehearsal, coach students to build strong connections within the ensemble in the process of the ritual. Perform each ritual for the group.
6. To create a performance piece, order the rituals and create transitions from one to the next. Rehearse and perform.

## CREATING SOLUTIONS

### Description
Working in small groups, students identify problems in their community and explore solutions through creating short scenes.

### Procedure
1. Have students brainstorm individually and write down ten problems they have observed in a common environment: school, family life, the community, the class, or a youth organization.
2. Write the ideas down on a board or big sheet of paper. Allow this sharing to generate even more ideas and record those as well.
3. Divide students into small groups. Direct the groups to sort the problems on the board into categories of their choosing and give each category an illustrative title.
4. Groups share with the class the categories they have developed.
5. As the first step to creating a performance from this exercise, each group does the following:

   Identifies one problem category with which to work.
   Identifies two different causes of their chosen problem.
   Imagines a solution to their chosen problem.
   Avoids stereotypes.
   Considers unexpected twists or explanations.
   Considers what part they play in this problem.
   Discuss what their solution requires of them.

6. Give each group fifteen minutes to fashion and rehearse a nonverbal performance piece to communicate the problem, root causes, and solutions they have identified. Their performances can include any or all of the following elements:

   taped music
   music from instruments played
   a symbolic object
   a piece of fabric
   nonverbal sounds
   poetry or narrative read by one member as the rest perform silently

   #### Coach as students work
   Get on your feet and try out your ideas.
   Involve everyone in your group equally.
   Take risks with your bodies.
   Make sure you are using facial expressions.

7. Each group's performance provides the class with excellent material for discussing the problems and solutions raised in class.

## TRIGGER SKITS

### Description

Trigger skits are short plays reflecting real-life situations. There is a story and a conflict, but no ending. The final scene is frozen at a heightened moment and the audience is engaged to help resolve the situation. Also known as interactive scene work, trigger skits were renamed by Central High students in the 1980s when original scenes were frozen the minute a gun was pulled and someone's finger was on the trigger.

### Considerations

The stories should evolve from personal and life experiences. Build carefully to the frozen moment so it invites a multitude of solutions.

### Procedure

1. Through brainstorming, discussion, and story sharing, have students decide on a theme or a focus for their work. Encourage them to make a choice based on what is most meaningful to them.
2. Choose groups of three to six students.
3. Each group is assigned to create a scene or series of short scenes that freezes at a climactic moment of conflict.
4. It may help to coach groups to work backward. First have them identify a climactic moment that illustrates their problem. Then have actors work backward in time from the climax to discover the history of the situation. Encourage exploration of many contributing points of view and social forces at work within their situation.
5. Each group outlines the scene that brings the chosen problem to life on stage.
6. After ample rehearsal, one group performs its scene through to the freeze ending for the rest of the class.
7. While the group performing holds its freeze, solicit resolutions for the scene from the audience. Coach the audience if needed.
8. Choose a single resolution or combine a number of the ideas suggested by the audience; then bring the scene to life so the actors can improvise the new ending.

## SHARED MONOLOGUES

### Description

Monologues, either original student creations or scripted pieces, can be explored creatively in small groups. The poem or the monologue becomes the script and the groups creatively design the presentation. Encourage students to integrate techniques and styles learned in beginning exercises, such as sculptures, vocal collaging, and movement. This activity could last several weeks.

### Procedure

1. Students read and study their group piece. Define who the character is, what the piece is about, and what it means to them; discuss the intent and ways to interpret and present the piece.
2. Next have students stand and experiment with different ways of presenting the monologue as an ensemble. Together students decide on the strongest way to present the monologue as a group and begin rehearsing for their presentation. Allow several days for rehearsal and development.
3. All students perform their shared pieces. Students can comment about what affected them in each piece and which choices were the more creative.

    *Variation 1: Solo Monologue Performances*
    After completing the ensemble work, individuals can work entire monologues on their own.

    *Variation 2: Solo Monologue with Ensemble Backup*
    One student works on a solo presentation of the text. The others work on interpreting the piece and creating a movement piece to perform with it. Movement can symbolize an internal monologue, a physicalization of the text, a force that works against or conflicts with the major theme, and so forth.

## SCULPTED SCENES ON THEMES

### Description

Students examine issues in their community by creating sculpted scenes and bringing them to life with words, action, and internal monologues created collectively by the group.

### Considerations

Students should be familiar with sculpting techniques. Have markers and large sheets of butcher paper on hand.

## Procedure

1. Students generate a list of themes to work with. For example:

   public education        violence
   discrimination          family conflict

2. In small or large groups, have students create a web chart with markers and paper that expands on the selected topic. The chart can include related words, situations, questions, feelings, related issues, stereotypes, song titles, or anything that comes to mind. Use the chart to help students expand their thinking about the topic and to elicit a wide range of feelings and perceptions, rather than try to be the most "correct."

   Build off each other's ideas.
   Take thinking in new directions.
   Remember, all ideas and suggestions are welcome.
   Offer ideas that are the opposite of what you think.

3. Have students look at the chart and think about images it may suggest. Students can enter and place themselves in the sculpture or be placed into the sculpture by their classmates.

4. Once the sculpture is complete, coach those in the sculpture to hold still and maintain their physical and emotional intensity. Then have the other student observers walk around it and try to imagine what each person is thinking.

   Look at each person's face. What are they thinking?
   Try to imagine the internal thoughts of each frozen character.

5. Next, have observing students stand beside a frozen character and speak their internal thoughts aloud.

   Select a character, stand near him or her, and speak their thoughts.
   Speak loud and with feeling.
   Enter and exit as many times as you want.

6. Finally, allow frozen characters to come to life in an improvised scene with dialogue, motivated by the internal monologues their classmates have given them. Leave time for discussion of issues that arise in this process.

## LONG-DISTANCE JOURNEYS

### Description
Students develop a small theatrical piece based on the concept of the questing tale, in which they embark on a demanding, imaginative journey in order to attain knowledge or enlightenment.

### Considerations
This exercise can be extended into a multiweek project.

> *Materials*
> butcher paper
> marker pens
> a selection of unusual music

### Day 1: Introducing the Journey
1. Begin a discussion by prompting students to generate a list of familiar "questing tales" or stories, movies, cartoons, or mythology in which a journey is taken.
2. As you discuss the questing tales, compare and contrast them until common elements emerge, such as the challenge, the obstacles, the fatal flaw, the interesting characters met along the way, the trickster.
3. Next identify morals and lessons in the questing tales.
4. Divide students into pairs. Have each pair together decide on an incident or crisis that can serve as the starting point for a questing journey.

    Two close friends get into a serious argument.
    A child is afraid to tell a parent something.
    A student fails to win an important scholarship.

### Day 2: Journey Maps
1. Divide students into project groups of five to six. Have each group brainstorm ideas for journeys and agree on one to explore.
2. Using markers and butcher paper, have each group draw the chosen journey using as much detail as possible. Coach students.

    Draw the paths your character must follow.
    Create the obstacles that your character must overcome.
    Think in terms of puzzles and mazes.
    Consider how magic can enter into your journey.

3. Once the maps are finished, have students tape them on the wall and then walk around and observe each other's maps.

### Days 3, 4, and 5: Act It Out

Have students improvise the opening scene, which should include an introduction of the central character(s), the conflict or problem they face, and the circumstances that instigate the journey. Using their maps as guides, have the groups complete their journeys in improvised mini-play form. Encourage students to include music, creative writing, dance, and movement as time and space allow. Perform scenes for each other.

## IMAGE CIRCLES

### Description

In this exercise, inspired by work of Augusta Boal, students take turns creating sculptures in the center of a circle as a way to communicate with one another about their feelings.

### Procedure

1. Begin by asking the entire group to form a circle.
2. Ask for three volunteers and have them stand in the center of the circle; they will be the "clay" to be sculpted.
3. Select a working theme. For instance:

   images in the media       pressures on the job       loneliness

4. The activity begins as one student from the circle walks to the center where the three volunteers stand in a neutral position. The student "sculpts" the three volunteers into an image inspired by the theme. When the sculpture is complete, the sculptor returns to the circle, and those in the sculpture hold the frozen image.
5. Students in the outside circle watch and react silently, then take turns sculpting the three volunteers in the middle into images reflecting different aspects of the theme.
6. The three volunteers in the middle remain frozen in the transition between sculptures. Explain to those being sculpted that if they get tired or just need a break they can step out and someone will replace them.
7. Coach the outer circle.
   Enter one at a time and respectfully sculpt your image.
   The image can be abstract or realistic.
   You do not need a plan; go with your instincts.
   Build on the image before or create an entirely new one.
   Take a few moments between sculptures so the group can react.
   If you need more than three people, add them from the circle.

8. Coach the students being sculpted.
   Work closely with classmates sculpting you.
   Maintain the emotional and physical posture.
   Keep breathing, stay relaxed.
   Build strong connections with others in the sculpture.
   If you feel fatigued, step out and someone will replace you.

9. When the exercise peaks, bring it to an end and repeat with another theme. You could also follow up with a writing exercise or discussion or continue a dialogue with images.

# CHAPTER FOUR

# Rehearsing

All in the same playing space must be in waiting while the unfolding of the drama takes place. Not *waiting for*, but *in waiting*. To wait is for the past or future. To stand in waiting is to allow the unknown—the new, the unexpected, perhaps the art moment—to approach.

VIOLA SPOLIN, *Theater Games for Rehearsal*

## Defining Rehearsal

Rehearsal is the endurance work of theatre. In its most basic form, it has actors repeat a piece over and over until it is performance-perfect. On the one hand, there is the expectation that each rehearsal will be identical; one of its main purposes is to produce memorization of lines and movements. On the other hand, the expectation is that each rehearsal will be an improvement over the one before it, because its other main purpose is to produce an audience-worthy show. Repetition is a building block of learning in any subject area: times tables, verb conjugations, important dates, music scales. In theatre, actors memorize the performance they will be executing. Plays performed from a script require word-for-word line memorization; if someone went to the trouble to write them, the actor goes to the trouble to memorize them, not get close or change them.

In improvised plays, where lines may vary ("This hurts me so much," might become "This hurts me deeply," or "I can't believe how much this hurts") actors must still commit to memory:

| | |
|---|---|
| line cues | entrances |
| exits | choreography |
| sequence | use of props |
| light cues | sound cues |

*[handwritten margin note: repetition as building block]*

The verb to rehearse is not a direct synonym for the verbs to repeat or to memorize; it carries with it the clear expectation of a performance to follow. The realization that they are preparing to stand up in front of others and perform produces the kind of anxiety revealed in the following small exchange. *prep to perform*

## CLASSROOM TRANSCRIPT: JENNIFER'S CLASS

### Preperformance Anxiety

It is seven days before my beginning drama class' final performance and we have begun the process of rehearsing the whole show at once. This means that some students are having to stand silently on stage while others perform for the first time. They can't talk to one another on stage or break character, and they are bored.

In addition, we are rehearsing for the second day on the auditorium stage rather than in my small classroom. The auditorium doubles as the cafeteria by day, and smells heavily of stale food. Giant fans are running to pump the greasy air outside, and the students must shout to be heard. I stand in the back of the auditorium and say "Louder!" when I can't hear an actor's line, which is almost every time someone speaks.

I tell the actors to take a five-minute break, except for the five kids who need to sharpen their memorization of a smaller scene. I approach the stage to be closer for this minirehearsal, and the following conversation takes place.

| | |
|---|---|
| STUDENT 1: | "Oh my God, when are we going to be done with this?" |
| JENNIFER: | "When this play is ready for an audience." |
| STUDENT 1: | "Do you think that will happen any time before the year 2000?" |
| JENNIFER : | "Not with an attitude like that I don't." |
| STUDENT 1: | "Seriously, how can you tell when it's ready?" |
| STUDENT 2: | "We're supposed to be able to feel it." |

*Performance not = Controlled ↓ rehearsal takes Control*

Unlike an exam, performance is not a controlled situation. Rehearsal's intention is to take control of the unfamiliar—the performance. When my students expressed doubts early on about their play, I could say calmly, "It will be great. By the time you get up there under the lights you will have done this a thousand times. You'll be able to perform this play in your sleep." But during rehearsals, they saw me insisting on their being better and better. For a shy student to say a line in a quavery voice for the first time is a big accomplishment, and one that earns a lot of praise in my class. But if no one in the opening night audience can understand her, then there is no reason for her to be on stage. So as rehearsals progress, she will hear me say over and over, "Louder please," "Even louder," "I can't hear you in the back row." Each time the student is being louder, but each time it still is not loud enough.

The combination of being too weary to rehearse a piece again and knowing the piece is still not good enough brings out the sarcastic, surly attitudes just illustrated. But Student 1's mouthy questions are quickly replaced by his real concerns:

> How will anyone know when it is good enough to perform?
> How can anyone be sure?
> What happens if we go out there thinking it's ready and it's not?

Student 2's response brings out another concern, that the act of repeating a piece over and over should not only improve it, but should also create in the performers an ability to judge it for themselves. Rehearsal should provide both intimate familiarity and overall perspective. Rehearsal is a demanding taskmaster.

*Rehearsal needs intimate familiarity & overall perspective*

Rehearsal is not just a time to repeat segments of the play; it revisits skills introduced earlier. For some time during the writing of this book, Jan puzzled over why she could not think of many exercises for rehearsing, even though she was aware of using them frequently in her classes. She realized that often during rehearsal she assesses weaknesses and redoes previous exercises. This poster defining rehearsing reflects its inclusion of receptive mind, ensemble, and creating components:

*You Are an Able Rehearser When You . . .*

- Take Direction
- Imagine What Is Not There
- Develop a Healthy Stamina
- Use a Sense of Humor
- Maintain Self-Discipline to Prepare Outside of Rehearsal

*1. Take direction*

Taking direction was the first skill both of us thought of when we began to discuss the rehearsal process. Taking direction is hard because it means accepting the need to do something differently or better. Perhaps taking direction is even harder for adolescents who spend a good amount of their time rebelling against authority figures in their quest for adulthood. But working in a program that advocates students communicating their own messages in original plays adds a third dimension. Up to the point of rehearsal, we as theatre coaches have spent most of our time convincing students that they can and should create their own ideas. We have listened, commented, and applauded.

During rehearsal, however, we wear the hat of a director and make decisions to guide the play to production. We do this for a number of reasons.

• Drama is an ensemble art, requiring the use of actors, technicians, designers, and musicians. It is an accepted practice that a director be appointed the person to coordinate all of these individual efforts under one final vision.

• We have been hired because we know more about the dramatic process than the young people with whom we work; by directing them we can pass what we know to them. Having acted in and directed more shows than they have gives us perspective and experience.

• We have been hired as schoolteachers. We are responsible for teaching district curricula, following school rules, and ultimately for the performance the students present to the public. In our minds, these two roles—the coach who encourages the emerging artist and the director who directs the emerging artist—are not in conflict, but every year we work hard to convince our students of this.

I begin the year with my drama students by posting all five of the defining posters on the walls of my classroom. I talk about the different roles I will play with my students. I tell them point blank that there will be times when I will watch the show and times when I will run the show. I explain that just as a professional director's job is to remain true to the intent of the playwright, my intent is to understand their creations and direct them faithfully. I listen carefully during the creation process and take notes. Even with this kind of careful preparation, teacher-directors face students who are insulted to receive direction, taking it personally or feeling that they are the only ones qualified to direct their own work.

For Jan, who brings many guest artists into her classroom, this resistance arises with guest directors as well. It also occurs when a student is assigned to be director for a day, or when small groups of students are rehearsing together and offering comments. We want our students to argue for what they believe in; we also want them to consider others' ideas. "Taking direction" means

> The hardest thing I do in here is be patient. It gets frustrating because it's hard work. People think it's easy in here. It's not. When scenes are being processed it's hard to do a scene over and over and over and over and over and over again. It seems like you're getting nowhere. You just have to say to yourself, "It's for a purpose."
>
> Tonicia, advanced acting student

not that students blindly do whatever they are told, but that they find appropriate ways to listen and respond to directions given.

The play the students were rehearsing in the preceding excerpt included a scene about an overweight girl being teased in gym, a scene that appeared performance-ready upon first improvisation, but in fact required extensive rehearsal before it could be presented to an audience.

## FIELD NOTE EXCERPT: JENNIFER'S CLASSROOM

### Rehearsing The Gym Scene

#### Creating the Scene

Earlier on in the playwriting process this ninth-grade class had brainstormed the problems that had faced them when they arrived at high school, and to my surprise they all agreed in their concern over how students treated one another in gym. They created a scene about an overweight girl teased by two boys. John expressed an eagerness to play the part of the head teaser, and in the first few versions delivered enough insults to make the scene realistic to his classmates.

#### First Day of Rehearsal

Once we moved into rehearsal, however, his insults increased in number and severity. Even though the intent of the scene was to stir some discomfort about how teens can treat one another, it was becoming too uncomfortable. The class audience was silent during the jokes, which had originally produced groans and chuckles. When I called John on veering from the original scene design, he challenged that he knew a lot more about what went on in gym class than I did.

No one else was defending John's changes, so I figured this was a personal, rather than ensemble, issue. "If I have to change it then I won't do it at all," John countered. Here I used something I had learned from Jan: "I'll think about it overnight if you will."

#### Second Day of Rehearsal

When John and I talked the next day, he said that he knew the barbs he had added during rehearsal were realistic because he had heard them directed at himself in elementary school. "That's why I had to play this part," he concluded, "because I know what it means to be the fat kid." I told John that I would like him to consider revealing his reasoning to his ensemble members; I thought they would be impressed and support him.

But I also asked John how he could draw the line between making the audience feel sympathy for the overweight character (played in fact by a quite thin girl from our class) and making himself feel powerful by taking on the role of the bully. He added that he thought he would eventually "get this out of his system." We agreed to keep the focus on the message of the scene with more jokes than had originally been written in, but also by placing a cap on how many he could add.

### Third Day of Rehearsal

In rehearsal the next day, the class was straightforward in asking how we had resolved the issue about John. In discussion about the issue, the class pointed to the ending of the scene as carrying part of the blame in sending the audience mixed messages. The original ending of the scene had the gym teacher step in and demand that the teasing stop, and recently John had begun mumbling more jokes under his breath to show that a teacher cannot force students to stop being mean to one another.

The rest of the class period was spent debating what would be the most realistic ending:

- a teacher stepping in and solving a problem
- the bully remaining in power as a bully
- the overweight girl stepping up and defending herself

The group of actors performing the scene would try out each version the class discussed, stopping and repeating as necessary to allow for the ideas being generated. *try out diff possible endings*

### Fourth Day of Rehearsal

At this point the ensemble at large was directing the rehearsal. The students asked their gym teacher to come to a rehearsal, and after watching carefully he asked that they not make the teacher look completely ineffective. He gave suggestions of what he might do in such a situation, and the girl playing the role of the gym teacher tried them out in front of him, so that he could coach for authenticity.

I liked the students' rehearsal process, but I also had an eye on the calendar; our performance date was too close for us to rewrite the whole play. When I told the students they had to solve the dilemma that day and move on, they decided to show all three possible endings to the audience with a narrator who says:

NARRATOR: (*stopping the action of the scene and walking down stage to address the audience*) After we created the problem in this scene, we couldn't figure out how to solve it. We've chosen three different endings; you choose. Take one! *Audience chooses!*

This rehearsal process required each of the elements on the rehearsal definition poster. Both John and I had to learn to take direction, to listen and consider and defer with respect to the person who knew more. The students as an ensemble had to take direction from me, from each other, and from the guest director. John's decision early on to change the scene in rehearsal resulted in his having to take more direction in the long run, so he taught his classmates a valuable lesson about the responsibilities that come with instituting change.

In rehearsal we ask students to imagine what it will be like to perform for an audience before they have done it. We also ask them to envision how a number of alternative approaches to a scene will look—will the line carry more weight if it is yelled, whispered, or said a with a sob at the end? Rehearsals cannot stop to make these decisions about every single line; instead, actors are expected to come to rehearsal both prepared and ready to think on their feet. Actors who have made the choice to prerehearse—to memorize, experiment, try it in front of a mirror—increase their rehearsal productivity.

My beginning students also showed healthy stamina in their rehearsal of the gym scene; they were willing to go back over the scene, the issues involved, and the alternative endings until they were satisfied that they had done their best. They persisted in asking questions—of John, of me, and of the gym teacher—and they showed the discipline to question themselves as well:

Did they have the best ending?

What were they communicating to their audience?

What did they want to communicate?

Choosing to revisit a snarled problem with the realistic goal, not of hitting on a magic solution, but of untangling it piece by piece, is itself a discipline that will serve students off the stage as well as on.

Once students recognize and experience the poster ingredients that make up an able rehearser, the scales printed below allow them to evaluate how accomplished they have become. This task forms an especially nice fit with the rehearsal process. The evaluative scales provide immediate feedback and also a metacognitive challenge. When students read and attempt to place themselves on the rehearsal continuums, they ask not only the question     *Evaluative process*

How well was I able to perform my part today?

but also

How well did I use rehearsal today to improve my performance?

A Student Is Rehearsing Well When a Balance Is Being Struck Between

| | |
|---|---|
| Accepting direction | Contributing constructive direction |
| Using competition to improve the play | Using cooperation to improve the play |
| Calling on endurance to repeat what has already been done | Calling on endurance to keep trying for new solutions |
| Knowing when to ask for help | Knowing when to take individual responsibility |
| Laughing at one's own mistakes | Taking one's own mistakes seriously |
| Remembering scripted lines and movements | Imagining a variety of viable alternatives |
| Recognizing failure | Recognizing success |

Jan has used these scales as the focal point of student-teacher conferences.

1. She and her interns discuss student strengths and weakness, comparing ideas to see if they are using the scales consistently.
2. Jan distributes a copy of the scales to each student and directs them to place themselves on the scales as honestly as possible. She then announces that at conference, students will explain their self-ratings, back them up with evidence, and that adults will do the same.
3. Students and adults meet one on one to discuss where the student is doing well and what areas require more learning. The scale evaluations on which the adult and student agree are then factored into the student's grade.

Jan likes the use of the scales in the grading process because of the responsibility it places on the student to self-evaluate. She notices a drop in student-teacher disagreements over evaluations since she has begun asking students not only to rate themselves, but also to look for evidence of their ratings.

In my class, students keep copies of the evaluative scales in their notebooks near their class journals. One or two days a week time is left at the end of class for students to write about what they have learned. Before they begin writing, we review the scales, and students document

*Student brings on scale*

evidence of their position on the continua as they come to mind. At the end of the grading period, students have an opportunity to look back over the scales on which they have recorded evidence and come to conclusions about what they have learned and what they still need to learn. Like Jan, I have noticed a decrease in student-teacher differences over evaluations. Having students collect evidence of their own learning gives them a clearer idea of what we do as teachers as well as a clearer picture of what they themselves have done.

## FIELD NOTE EXCERPT: JAN'S CLASSROOM

### Rehearsing a Meeting with the Principal

#### The Problem

During my fourth visit to Jan's classes in Minnesota, the school was experiencing a policy shake-up. Students could be seen wandering the halls with increasing frequency when they should have been in class. Teachers used to a well-disciplined school were becoming increasingly annoyed.

After consulting the faculty and the PTA, the administration made the decision to come down hard on students out of class. Over the loudspeaker the principal announced to the students that teachers were being instructed to lock their doors at the bell. Any students found in the hall after the lock-down would be "swept" and sent to an in-school detention for a first offense and suspended at the second offense. Some students I spoke to agreed that tough consequences were the best approach to getting kids to class, but the majority I observed from Jan's classroom thought the new policy outrageously unfair.

#### The Reaction *Policy Changes*

As I walked through the bottom-floor halls in the mornings I heard heated discussions analyzing how recent increases in enrollment had clogged the halls, making it impossible to get anywhere on time; questions about whether or not it was fire-safe to have locked doors in a school; declarations of various parents' (and students') intentions to sue; and clear opinions that the policy was a racist strategy for suspending black students.

The day after the new policy announcement, a group of Jan's advanced acting students came to the drama room at break to discuss the situation. I was in the room by myself, trying to catalogue some tapes and waiting for Jan to return from a meeting. It was not hard for me to hear the students' heated conversation, and they could plainly see me in the room.

One young man, Levi, seemed to be the most upset and ready for action. He actually had brought with him some signs, hand-drawn on the backs of old assignment sheets, which read:

Central High: A Prison for Everyone (with jailhouse illustration)
You Could be Suspended Just for Going to You're [sic] Locker!

When he had a free moment, I walked over and asked if he would be interested in telling me on the tape recorder what he was up to.

### The Idea

"We'll demand that the principal change the policy before we come back," he assured me.

"Do you think that will work?" I asked. "And, well, what if she won't talk to you? Aren't you just going to make her mad?"

"So? We're already mad. So are our parents, too, and if they don't change that rule, they're gonna be sorry."

"Why don't you just go to her office and tell her what's on your mind?" I asked. The principal, whom I had met and interviewed on several occasions, struck me as an especially fair-minded and intelligent woman who, until now, students had liked. She was very supportive of Jan's program and the many unconventional things they did.

"I don't know what I'd say," he hesitated.

Jan and I had been talking a lot about rehearsal during this visit, and I was curious as to why Levi was neglecting all that he knew as an advanced acting student about the importance of rehearsal.

"So plan it out before you go in," I offered.

"There's no time; everybody's ready to do this now."

I could see Levi debating in his mind: to pull off the walkout protest and get the satisfaction of immediacy or wait and try the in-office conference.

"We could still walk in carrying the signs," he imagined out loud.

"And she's going to think to herself that no student who is following the rules will be suspended for going to their locker," I said, pointing to one of his signs, "and you spelled 'your' wrong."

> In here I am learning to work together even with people who may be difficult to work with, and learning that if we don't do it together, we fall apart.
>
> Michelle, beginning acting student

Levi looked at me. Nothing is more annoying than an overzealous English teacher. Jan walked in and raised an eyebrow at us, but said nothing.

"Like doing a play," I said, "figure out what you're going to say, practice it, then do it for other people."

"OK, but you be the principal," he challenged.

## The Rehearsal  *Role-play*

We spent about an hour with me playing an adult in authority and Levi trying out different approaches to getting the suspension and lockdown rules changed. I rarely spoke outside of my character, and it wasn't necessary for me to do so. Levi was such an experienced actor and rehearser that he could pick up the feedback he needed from my "character's" remarks alone. He directed himself, using my reactions as constructive criticism.

## The Solution

That night he talked to his grandmother about what she thought would be best for him to do. The next morning he went to the principal's secretary and made an appointment to speak with her that afternoon with three other students. He and his fellow students spent forty minutes talking to the principal in her office, and at the end of their conversation she promised the students she would bring their ideas for a softer discipline policy to the faculty.

With some modifications, the new three-strikes policy was adopted one week later. When I talked to the principal about the situation, she revealed that the night before Levi came to her office, she had been at a community meeting where parents and students became angry about the situation and even yelled at her. "I had to sing hymns in the car on the way home to calm myself down," she recalled, laughing. "I already knew something would have to change before those kids came in here, but the way they presented themselves, I was glad to listen to them."

When I asked Levi about it he said, "It was pretty cool. It went like I planned."

Levi took the responsibility for the success of his idea, through bringing the idea up with others (both students and adults), debating it, and rehearsing it. Although I was more intrusive in this situation than I usually was with Jan's students, Levi clearly used me as a tool to help himself accomplish his goal.

## Using Rehearsal  *Performing is complex task*

Productive rehearsal serves to remind students of the difficulty of their task. Standing up in front of an audience and performing is a complex task, and its success rests on a web of variables.

Is each actor loud enough?
Is each actor visible to the audience?
Is all memorization in place?
Do actors know their characters deeply enough?
Do actors interact with one another naturally?
Do the actors observe their technical cues?
Do the actors observe proper timing and pace?

What follows is an assignment for the drama classroom designed to allow students to review and repeat their work to bring it to performance quality. The unit begins by introducing students to the trigger skit—a short, flexible script that can be applied to any number of situations, such as:

A: Hey.
B: What are you doing?
A: It's complicated.
B: Well, I think I should know.

Students pair up and bring their own creative interpretation to the script. During performance, everyone sees the same scene repeated over and over, as well as a new scene with each performance, determined by the actors' inflections, movements, and expressions. This trigger skit could take place, for example, between a chief mechanic who resents a new hire and an eager new employee, or between a worried mom who is looking through her daughter's drawers and the angry daughter who interrupts her. Once students grasp the idea of a trigger skit, they can create their own trigger scripts and offer them to the ensemble for a performance test drive. The success of a trigger skit script quickly reveals itself when assigned to a collection of paired actors; if all pairs end up performing basically the same interpretation, the script is too limiting in its dialogue.

For this assignment, I have my students pair up and expand a skit into a full-length scene. Students devise their initial script drafts in a number of ways:

talking back and forth about ideas
getting up and improvising a scene
outlining and then writing the script

Whichever the creation method, the following assignment sheet makes clear that they will be expected to return to and review their original idea several times.

## CLASSROOM ASSIGNMENT: JENNIFER'S CLASSROOM

### *The Trigger Skit Project*

### Trigger Skit Scenes

It's time for your second big performance in drama. This time you will be performing with another person in a scene that you will write together. Here are the guidelines to follow for writing your scene:

———— Your scene should be based on and include one of the four trigger skits you were provided with.

———— Your scene should expand on the trigger skit of your choice to two or three pages in length.

———— Your scene should begin with a brief paragraph that explains who your characters are and what your setting is.

———— Your scene should have a beginning, middle, and end.

———— Your scene should include a minimum of eighteen stage directions indicating what your characters will do with their bodies, faces, props, and emotions.

———— Your scene should include the use of one prop by each character.

———— Your scene should be written like a play, with characters' names in the margin, a colon after their names, stage directions in parentheses, and lines written on the page without quotation marks. For examples, see the green folder.

———— The final copy of your scene should be neatly presented in ink or, better yet, typed or word-processed. Check the guidelines for handing in a paper in your handbook.

———— You should have three copies of your scene to hand in on the due date—one for each of you and one for me.

———— Each of you should complete a response sheet for your scene at home and hand it in with your scene. Completed response sheets will be worth 25 points to each person.

———— Your completed scene will be due on Thursday for 100 points. Both of you will share this grade.

This assignment requires students to

- write or improvise a first draft     2 drafts
- write a second draft observing the conventions of scriptwriting
- write a third draft taking into account the comments of the classmates, the teacher, and an outside reader
- write a final draft that is proofread, extremely neat, and suitable for submission.     4 drafts total

This process of creating and rehearsing requires time; students cannot be expected to produce this many drafts and have the perspective necessary to review them without time. This performance assignment began with the trigger skit:

What are you doing?
Something I should have done a long time ago.
But you can't.
Why?
Because.
Think about it.

This class of ninth graders was particularly compelled by issues of peer pressure: They had heard of the phrase before coming to high school, but now that they were here they were surprised by the difficult realities of being pressured by classmates. One group improvised the following script on their first try:

SARAH:     What are you doing, Jesus?
JESUS:     Something I should have done a long time ago.
MONICA:     But you can't.
JESUS:     Why?
MONICA:     Because.
SARAH:     Think about it.
JESUS:     I know what I'm doing.
SARAH:     Think about your family. Think about the consequences.
JESUS:     It's about me. Stay out of it.
MONICA:     Don't talk to her like that.
SARAH:     We're tying to help you.
JESUS:     Stay out of my life. I don't care what goes on—it's stupid. It's my problem. I don't need this. If you really want to help, loan me some money and then leave me alone.
MONICA:     For what?
SARAH:     I'm not going to give you money for drugs.
JESUS:     Fine, if you're not going to give me money I'll get it from somewhere else.

| SARAH: | Leave then. |
| MONICA: | Wait—don't go. I'll give you the money, but only five bucks. |
| SARAH: | Don't do that! |
| MONICA: | Sarah, shut up! |

To help with perspective, students are required to bring the script they draft to someone outside the classroom for comments. This group of three collared an older brother to fill out their response sheet, and it provides an example of how what seemed clear to the creators did not come across as clearly to a reading audience.

### Response Sheet: The Trigger Scene

*Dear Family and Friends:*

*Thank you very much for taking the time to read your student's work. For this assignment, drama students paired up and selected trigger skits—brief six-line skits that could be said by just about any character in any setting—to expand into the two- or three-pages scene that you are about to read. These scenes should dramatize a conflict between two characters and keep your interest. Enjoy reading!*

1. What did you enjoy the most about this scene?
   When Jesus comes back and asks the girls for money. They were supposed to be helping him, but by giving him money, I don't think they are.
2. What are some questions you have about this scene?
   The beginning, when Sarah asks, "What are you doing Jesus?" It's confusing because it doesn't explain what he is doing. From that line it's hard to grasp or get an idea about the topic, until the middle.
3. Anything else you'd like to say?
   No!                                               Charles Garfia, 11-20

Next, the three ninth graders revised the rough draft of their scene, not only addressing the respondent's concerns, but also changing their ending. The student authors decided it would be more effective to leave the audience wondering what would happen next, as opposed to spelling out the ending with the all-out fight they had first envisioned.

Once students have completed the script portion of the scene, they must prepare it for performance. In my classroom, this process requires word-for-word memorization of the script. I give students several days, with some time in class and some out of class, to practice their memorization. I call on students to complete a memorization drill in which I hold their scripts and they prove that they have memorized accurately.

The completion of this stage signals the beginning of what most people think of as rehearsal. With the help of the types of exercises listed in this chapter, we review students' characters, movements, timing, risk taking, and overall performance plan. At this point, it is conceivable that students have repeated their scene scripts as many as one hundred times. Students also rehearse for guest directors outside of our classroom, using a sheet similar to a response sheet. This time this group sought out a student teacher as their guest director.

They asked to use my room at lunch for their rehearsal, and to my surprise the student teacher had them repeat the scene three times. He explained that he needed to see it more than once to be able to comment completely. He also had a few ideas for them to try. As I watched, the student complained, "Ms. Wolf, he's making us do it over and over!" Mr. Thurber's comments on the guest director sheet prove to the actors that concerns about risk taking, commitment, and visibility on stage belong to more than one person.

### Guest Director Sheet: The Trigger Scene

*Dear Family and Friends:*

*Thank you very much for taking the time to watch this performance. For this assignment, students have had to work together to write their own two- or three-person scene, memorize their lines, and plan how to perform their characters and movements on stage. When the students perform this scene, they will be graded on how easily they can be understood and how many dramatic risks they take with characters and emotions. Your comments will help these students to improve their final performance. Enjoy the show!*

1. What did you enjoy the most about watching this scene?
   The message is strong.
   Good blocking.
   Body language is convincing.
   Excellent script.
   It flowed well.
2. What would you like to see more or less of in this scene? Why?
   Slow down, try to feel it first, then say it.
   Have a concerned, yet controversial tone.
   Sarah, pause more, between every line.
   Jesus, act more righteous.
   Monica, your facial expressions, tie back your hair.
3. What final directorial comment would you like to offer?
   Take it easy, feel it, say it, mean it.               Mr. Thurber, 12-12

## Learning from Rehearsal

Original play work with students can contribute a certain fear factor to the rehearsal process. With a professionally written play the director can at least have faith in the script's audience-tested appeal, even if actors are struggling in rehearsal, but an original script renders every aspect of performance unknown. In the following tape-recorded conversation, Jan tells me a story that reinforces the importance of taking risks in rehearsal.

## TRANSCRIPT: JAN

### The Risks of Rehearsing Original Work

Sometimes rehearsal blues come because the content of the play isn't working. Sometimes you have to revamp the whole play. We did one play about shoes in intermediate drama. The kids gave up on it and they attacked me in front of an audience!

The kids who came to watch it for a preview performance rolled their eyeballs, and . . . well, they didn't like it. One actor stood up after the play and told the audience, "This wasn't our idea anyway, this was *Jan's* idea." I just sat there, and I said, "Oh? Let's hear more about this." They started to debate and then the bell rang and everybody left. They didn't want to do this play anymore.

So the next day I asked, "Well, what do you want to do? We don't have to do this." I said that if anybody really wanted to try to restructure the whole plot, then they should come in at lunch.

So, Nick and Cody and Eli and a few other people came in and we figured out that we needed a narrator because the story was confused and needed focus. It was great because they were right. After we figured that out I said, "Let's stage it." Well, in those following two and a half weeks of rehearsal the play went from forty-five minutes of confusion to ten minutes of something good.

And that's the risk of doing original work; it ain't always great. But it's about problem solving; it's not about making perfect work. Every three or four years, there's just something that comes up stinky; it just isn't quite right.

*They can learn something from observing. So often, I'll give them an assignment and say, "I'm going to be directing this, and I want you to think of whether you'll make choices similar or different to what I'm doing. Jot down some notes about it." And afterward I'll ask, "What did you think? Do you agree or disagree?" So you give them a little task, because the watching part is really hard for them.*

≠ problem solving over perfection

Even though it was awkward to have all that criticism come toward me, I'm glad that I was a fifteen-year veteran teacher, or I probably would have gone home and cried. But I was able to remove myself and watch them deal with it. And it ended up that when they performed it in front of the whole school audience, people loved it.

## Rehearsal Warm-ups

The following activities enhance the rehearsal process with techniques to keep the energy fresh during the repetitive process of polishing a piece for performance.

### Exercises for Stage Presence

### SILENT SPEED-THROUGH TO MUSIC

Have students run through the entire show quickly and silently to music. Remind cast not to skip any beats of action, but instead, to focus on heightening the energy, exaggerating the characters, picking up the pacing, and making distinct entrances and exits.

### ENTRANCES AND EXITS

Ask students to enter the stage one at a time with the rest of the class watching. Before entering, the actor must justify the entrance.

> Round one: What room are you coming from?
> Round two: Where are you going?
> Round three: What just happened?

Each actor enters, walks across the stage, and freezes before exiting. The class tries to guess the circumstances. Follow up with a rehearsal focusing on energizing entrances and exits.

### STAGE PICTURE

As the entire group moves randomly around the stage, coach for risk and variety in the movement. Call out "Freeze" and direct students to quickly create a stage picture in which everyone can be seen. Begin another round, add music, or layer on emotions or characters. Once again call "Freeze" and have students quickly create a frozen picture that highlights all actors equally.

### MIRRORS CHANGING PARTNERS

Students get in partners and begin a basic mirror exercise without designating a leader. Partners create simultaneous movement by staying connected and working together. When you give the signal to change,

*Stage Picture*

everyone leaves their partners—very slowly, without breaking the rhythm—and finds another partner by establishing eye contact and mirroring together. The partner can be someone close by or someone on the other side of the room. Allow students to change partners several times.

### Exercises for Boosting Energy

## SOUND TAG

Similar to Chain Tag except participants have eyes closed and make soft sounds. Moving slowly in the space, IT finds others by listening to their sounds. As IT captures classmates one by one, they all stay together, slowly capturing the entire group. This is best done outside or in a large room.

## COSTUME RELAY

Line up two or three teams in relay lines. Provide each team with a simple costume—for example, a hat, glasses, scarf, and jacket. Instruct the first person in each line to put on the costume, run to the goal and back, remove the costume, and help dress the second person, who must continue the relay. The game ends when everyone runs the relay path in full costume.

## REHEARSAL RUN, FREEZE, AND FOCUS

The repetition of rehearsal can create stress, boredom, or weariness. Be flexible enough to stop for a moment and change gears. Have students jog around in the space; then yell "Freeze" and have them stretch slowly to music. Have them run again; when you yell "Freeze" have them all shout out how they feel. Again have students jog; then yell "Freeze" and instruct them to focus on their hands, on the ceiling, on their breathing, or on the music. Move them around to shake off the distractions, then transition back to the task.

## FORWARD AND REVERSE SCENE WORK

To help students memorize lines and blocking, practice rehearsing one scene (an active scene works best, or have actors exaggerate movement). While the scene is in progress call out "Reverse" and have students play out the scene backward, retracing their steps, and saying their lines in reverse order. Next call out "Forward," and the action moves forward until someone calls out "Reverse." This process can help lock in lines and also provide comic release in the rehearsal process.

## PARTNER TAG TO SCENES

To play Partner Tag students move in pairs instead of moving individually. When a pair is tagged, the partners explode into an exaggerated frozen pose together. Once everyone is frozen, ask students to bring their body position to life in an improvised scene. Part of the students' challenge is to negotiate spontaneously which partner's idea will evolve into a scene. For the next round, have partners play the game as their play characters.

### *Exercises for Vocalization*

## CIRCLE LINE REHEARSAL

Have the cast stand in a big circle and have each actor select one line from his or her scene. For round one, each student calls out his or her lines at the same time. For round two, each student adds a body movement to match the line. For round three, each actor performs his or her line, one at a time, and the entire group repeats it back. Rotate around the circle until everyone has performed a line, with the ensemble echoing back each line like a group mirror.

## VOCAL PROJECTION AND INTERPRETATION

Have each student select one line from the play to work with, then ask students to choose partners. Instruct students to take turns saying this one line to each other as many times and with as much variety as possible. Encourage them to coach each other for volume, honesty, energy, physicality, and depth. Have everyone get in a circle and allow each student to perform his or her line in several ways.

### Exercises for Character Development

## WHAT I AM NOT

As students walk in the door, hand each a card with instructions that reads "Begin creating a character who you are not." Give students a short amount of time to create characters with qualities vastly different from their own. Keep students walking so you can coach them and allow them to build from the physical into other personality aspects of the character. Invite the characters into a circle and have them introduce themselves one at a time. Feel free to ask them questions to help them further explore and define their characters.

## CHARACTER STUDIES

Write the names of all your students on small pieces of paper and place them in a hat or box. As soon as students walk in the room, have them select a name but not reveal that name to anyone. Instruct students to study carefully the physicality of that person, including walk, habits and mannerisms, and manner of sitting. Give students three to four days for this observation. For closure, have each person make an entrance and sit down as the person they observed and have the class try to guess who it is.

## CHARACTER ROTATIONS

To bring new life to a play, have students play each other's characters. Or, focus on one scene and let the entire cast take turns playing one specific role.

## BODY CONVERSATIONS

Ask students, working in partners, to identify characters and a conflict and begin improvising a scene. Freeze the scenes and instruct students to continue the argument in silence using only a given body part; for example, ask them to argue with their hips, with their faces, or with their hands. Finally, instruct them to have the conversations with the entire body, adding sounds or gibberish.

## GROUP INTERVIEW

Two or three students sit in chairs facing the class. Classmates ask them questions to help them further define their characters. The students being interviewed must remain in character and answer all questions honestly. After a short interview, new characters sit in the chair for an interview. Depending on the topic, the interview might take the form of, for example, an interrogation, a trial, or a talk show.

## BIOGRAPHIES

Using stories, letters, or journal entries, have students write a short biography of their character. Offer questions that guide students to think about the character's childhood memories, significant events, and family relationships.

*Sometimes if things drag, like in the middle of March, we do relays for ice cream, or something fun, to get them out of their heads. Or I give them a time limit: "You can only have ten minutes to rehearse these things and then we're going to perform them all."*

# Rehearsal Techniques for Enhancing a Specific Scene

Select one scene on which to focus and apply several of the techniques listed for actors to explore and expand characters and story.

### Images in Motion

Have students divide the scene into four sections and create still images representing each part. Encourage the use of exaggerated gestures, props, and visual symbols to communicate subtext. For example, if a character has a higher status than others in the scene, that character might stand on a table. Ask the audience for feedback on to how to improve each image. After students have created the four consecutive images as described, have them rehearse their entire scene in large, animated movements that communicate the story and the characters in picture and gesture only (no words).

### Internal Monologues

Have students begin rehearsing the scene; at any point call out "Freeze." Actors must hold their positions and immediately begin speaking an internal monologue that reveals all the thoughts inside of the character's head. Have characters return to the action of the scene by calling "Go." Freeze the action at any time to allow students to deepen their characters and explore the dynamics at any moment of the scene.

### Stop and Style

Students begin rehearsing the scene. Any classmate in the audience can freeze the action at any time and call out a genre, such as musical comedy. Actors must continue the scene in that style until someone else freezes the action and suggests another genre, such as opera. Remind students that the blocking and the text of the scene should not change.

### Freeze and Justify

Begin the scene rehearsal. Any classmate can call out "Freeze" and halt the action at any time and pose a question to one of the actors. For example, a question to someone playing a mother character might be, "Why don't you have more sympathy for your daughter?" A question to the daughter might be, "Why is there so much anger in your tone of voice right now?" The student playing the character must explain and defend choices of tone and action.

## *Motivation Switch*

Have students run the scene once. Then have classmates suggest a single emotion, such as fear, and have the actors run the scene once again with fear as the primary motivation for all characters. For a second round, select a contrasting emotion, such as love, and run the scene again. Coach actors not to change the text or improvise new lines. The only thing that changes is the motivating emotion.

## Exercises for Teaching Rehearsal

### ANIMAL CHARACTERS

#### Description
Students transform from an animal to a human to create or deepen characters.

#### Procedure
1. Students sit in a circle and generate a list of animals.
2. One student volunteers to go to the center of the circle and is assigned an animal.
3. Coach the student to take on the characteristics of this animal while they are within the performance space.

   Now that you are a fox your body is covered with fur.
   You have very sharp teeth.
   You are walking with paws instead of feet.
   How do your eyes move?
   You have a tail.
   Imagine your nose jutted out; the tip of it is cold.
   Is this fox hungry? Agitated?

4. Once the student feels comfortable physically with the animal posture, coach him or her through a gradual transformation from the animal to a person who may have qualities similar to the animal.
5. Once the character appears, ask questions along with the other students to help define and explore the nature of this new character. The character responds, maintaining qualities of the original animal, such as voice, posture, and pace.

   What's your name?
   How old are you?
   Who is your best friend?
   What do you do for a living?
   How are you feeling right now?
   Describe a room in your house.
   Do you have children?
   What has been the best event in your life? The worst?

6. Proceed through the circle of students.
   *Variation: Creating Scenes*
   Once a character is brought to life, invite in a second actor and create a scene.

## EXPLORING THE LIFE OF CHARACTERS

### Description
Because improvisational acting develops material quickly, characters can lack depth and history. This activity requires students to explore the lives and histories of characters in their scenes. It generates new material and keeps the process fresh.

### Procedure
1. Have students pair off and choose Partner A and Partner B.
2. Partner A briefly describes his or her play character to Partner B.
3. Together the partners imagine an episode or moment from this character's life not included in the play, and improvise a scene around it.

   Create a memory from the character's past.
   Push time ahead and create a scene in the character's future.
   Reveal a conversation the character has with his conscience.
   Explore an important moment or a special day.
   Discover a moment that might explain your character's intentions.
   Reveal an interaction with a friend, relative, or stranger.
   Bring to life a dream or fantasy the character might have.

4. Perform scenes for the class and discuss the accuracy and relevance of the scene.
5. Reverse and have Partner B's character be the focus of a scene.
   *Variation: Random Meeting*
   Partners create a scene that allows both of their characters to meet or interact.

## EXTENDED ENVIRONMENT

### Description
Extended environments invite students to create characters and enter a defined situation for a substantial period of time, from thirty minutes to

over an hour. This allows for the deep exploration of character and builds the endurance necessary to sustain focus and concentration.

## Procedure:

1. Explain to students that they will be participating in extended improvisation and briefly set the ground rules.

   You will be improvising for the entire class period.
   It is very important not to break character at any time.
   Focus on the give and take between characters.
   Don't let any one person become the center of attention.
   Your character must have an active and interactive presence.
   Playing tired or passive the entire time is not OK.
   Make choices that heighten tension or move action forward.
   Allow your character to take risks.

2. Describe the environment and have students create characters or use their play characters. On command have students enter and establish a setting:

   | a support group | a school dance | a Greyhound bus depot |
   | the airport | a stuck elevator | a tribal village |

   and begin interacting with each other.

3. The teacher can be a character in the improv or can merely observe. To move the action forward, heighten the conflicts, or circumvent unproductive events in the improvisation, freeze the action and talk to the characters. Feel free to change time, location, or add additional information.

4. With about ten minutes remaining, choose an appropriate place to freeze the action of the improv. After the freeze, ask students to sit quietly, close eyes, and reflect on the extended improvisation they have just finished, then write a poem or monologue about the experience.

   *Variation: Generating Written Material*
   Ask the students to write a letter to someone related to their character describing what their character felt or did during the extended improvisation.

## ENSEMBLE CHARACTER WALK

### Description

This exercise is designed to help students explore the external and internal life of their characters.

## Procedure

1. Begin with a walking meditation, coaching students to relax, focus on their breathing, and let go of thoughts and tensions.
2. Coach students to transform slowly into their character, beginning with their body.

   Physically transform into your character.
   What part of your body leads—the head, shoulders, stomach?
   Does your character move slower or faster than you do?
   Modify your posture.
   Explore the muscles in your face.
   How old are you? Feel your age. Let it affect your body.

3. Coach students to choose a moment from a scene for their character to focus on and to feel the emotions in that scene.

   Let these emotions affect your face, your hands, your muscles.
   What thoughts are going through your character's mind?
   Let the mind wander.
   Let the body react.
   Your feelings will affect your breathing.

4. Coach students to pause and let their characters begin an activity spontaneously with a pantomimed object, such as washing dishes or packing a suitcase.

   Heighten the feeling and let it affect the action.
   Keep moving.
   Don't stop to plan.
   Go with your instincts.

5. Finally, ask students to continue the activity and begin to whisper the inner thoughts of the character in a spontaneous monologue.
6. Close by inviting all students to stand in a circle in character.
   Have students share a short moment of their inner monologues.
   Tap students one at a time on the shoulder as the signal to speak.

## HATS, SCARVES, AND PROPS

### Description

This activity challenges students to rapidly establish character using costume pieces and simple props.

### Considerations

Collect hats, fabric, and simple props such as glasses, stuffed animals, artificial flowers, and baskets. Divide them into piles or boxes.

## Procedure

1. Begin by selecting small group teams of four to six students.
2. Have students sit together with their team.
3. Select one team to go first. This team stands together in front of the class.
4. The class calls out a "Where."

   park     kitchen     toy store     basement     library

5. This team is given only two minutes to select costume pieces and define a scene that would take place in the given location.
6. Have the entire class count down the last ten seconds to performance.
7. Each team takes a turn preparing a scene in two minutes.
8. For round two, have each team pick five costume pieces for another team. The costumes pieces are set in the playing area. This time the costumes alone must serve as the inspiration for the scene.

   *Variation: More Specific Where*
   Ask teams to further define the Where. For example:

   a park in England     a kitchen in heaven
   a toy store on the moon     a Braille library

## UNDERSTANDING INTENTION

### Description

Students explore contrasting intentions in a given text using simple nursery rhymes.

### Procedure

1. Have students get into groups of four.
2. Each group selects a short nursery rhyme to work with.

   Twinkle, Twinkle Little Star    Row, Row, Row Your Boat
   Itsy Bitsy Spider            Little Boy Blue

3. Have the four students divide up the lines so that each has one line.

   A: Twinkle, twinkle little star, how I wonder what you are.
   B: Up above the world so high, like a diamond in the sky.
   C: Twinkle, twinkle little star.
   D: How I wonder what you are.

4. Next hand out a list of intentions.

to apologize       to bore        to frighten       to excite
to shock           to plead       to intimidate     to forgive
to entertain       to shame       to flatter        to tease

5. Instruct each small group to select four contrasting intentions and assign them so that each person will deliver a line motivated by a different intention.

   A: (to intimidate)
   B: (to flatter)
   C: (to entertain)
   D: (to bore)

6. Have groups perform their nursery rhyme as a four-part monologue highlighting each person and the contrasting intentions.

## RESISTANCE MOVES

### Description

Resistance moving is random slow-motion exercise in which bodies move through space while resisting it. This work encourages exploration of feeling through slow and deliberate movement.

### Procedure

1. Begin by having students move through the room quickly, exploring space with their bodies.
2. Slow the movements down and suggest that students imagine that the space through which they are moving is getting thicker.

   The air is thick with humidity.
   Now the air is the consistency of glue, soft butter, thick clay.

3. Coach movement until students attain a clear and consistent focus, resisting the air with all the muscles in their bodies.

   Resist the air with your face, your fingers, your back.
   Keep breathing; stay relaxed.

4. Next have students choose a character to work with from their scene or play. Have them focus on an emotionally charged moment in the play.
5. Coach them to become an emotion inside of their character, and move through space as the emotion.

   Select an emotion driving your character.

Remember, you are the feelings inside the person, not the person.
Become the rage, the love, the fear.
Maintain the strength of the resistance; move.
Intensify your struggle with the thickness of the air.
Keep the feelings circulating through your entire body.
Open your eyes.
Make contact with others.
Welcome all emotions.
Allow one emotion to transform into another.

6. Let students explore the emotions inside their characters in different situations in the play or scene.
7. After the last character exploration, allow students to slowly stretch, relax, and release the feelings of the exercise. Or, direct them immediately to a writing exercise and have them express the feeling as a poem or monologue.

## EMOTION MIRRORS

### *Description*
Concentration work in pairs helps to express and share emotions. This entire exercise is done in silence. Once students connect with their own emotions, coach them to transfer appropriate emotions to the lives of their characters.

### *Procedure*
1. Students stand in pairs, face to face, choosing a Partner A and Partner B.
2. Partners close their eyes, drop their heads, and breathe until they are relaxed.
3. Instruct Partner A to choose a strong emotion on which to focus. Coach Partner A to begin to feel emotion internally and slowly, then begin to make it visible externally through body language and facial expression.
4. When the ensemble attains ability to focus, have everyone open their eyes. Coach Partner A to maintain the emotion.
5. Partner B's task is to carefully observe, understand, and mirror back the emotion Partner A is silently communicating. This exercise need not be one of gross physical movement; coach for subtle and intense movements.

Let the emotion extend to every part of your body.
Don't move.
Remember a time in your life when you experienced this feeling.
Let the feeling build until it feels strong enough to burst out.

6. Walk around the room and observe students while coaching them.

   Maintain the intensity of emotions.
   Feel energy flowing between you.
   Maintain eye contact.
   Keep breathing.

7. Have partners switch places.
   *Variation 1: Speaking the Heart*
   Encourage students to softly express to their partners, this time in words, how they feel.
   *Variation 2: Scene Start-up*
   One person speaks. This line serves as the beginning of a scene between the two.

## SOUND AND MOVEMENT FOLLOW AND LEAD

### Description
Students communicate and express feelings through sound and movement only. Follow this exercise by a run-through of the entire play in sound and movement only.

### Procedure
1. Have students make a large circle, and ask for a volunteer to lead.
2. The leader stands in the center of the circle and creates a series of movements and sounds. The rest of the class spontaneously follows along, reflecting the movements and sounds like a group mirror. Coach the leader to explore a wide range of sound, emotion, and movement. Coach the group to strive for unity as they mirror the leader's actions.
3. Leadership can be transferred to another classmate by the leader making a sound and gesture toward another person, who then begins his or her own series of sound and movement activities. Repeat until everyone has had a turn leading.
   *Variation 1: Add Themes*
   Side coaching can guide movement into specific themes.

   power      jealousy      paranoia      sympathy

*Variation 2: Call and Response*
The leader chooses an emotion and makes sounds representing that emotion. The group moves to those sounds for a short period of time, then tries to guess the emotion. This can be reversed, having the leader choose an emotion and create movement to represent the feeling while the rest of the group makes sounds.

*Variation 3: Conductor*
In small groups, students create a ten-second sound and movement piece on a selected theme. Have them design an easily repeatable piece. When sound and movement phrases are complete, gather groups in a large semicircle and select a conductor to lead the group. The conductor brings each phrase to life and can start and stop them to create any effect desired.

## INTERACTIVE SCENE WORK FOR REHEARSAL

### Description
Interactive scene work takes place during rehearsal when a scene is frozen and the student audience takes turns replacing the characters and replaying the action. The scene can be replayed several times, allowing students to participate and offer a variety of solutions to the problem presented. What begins as an individual problem becomes the responsibility of the group and an expression of the group's creativity.

### Procedure
1. Have students agree upon a scene that needs work.
2. Instruct students to improvise the scene.
3. On impulse, students in the audience yell "Freeze." At this point the focus character leaves the scene and is replaced by a student from the audience. The action can be backed up to the start of the scene or continue from where it left off.
4. The scene is replayed and the actor from the audience presents a new interpretation of the character's actions until another student yells "Freeze."
5. Continue the interactive rehearsal process, drawing on the creativity of the entire class to enhance scenes and characters.
6. Finally, the original cast reworks the scene incorporating the input of the group.

## TUG OF WAR SCENE

### Description
This exercise provides students with a physical metaphor for conflict on stage. This process will also reveal how well the characters are listening and responding to each other and where the scene drags or becomes repetitive.

### Considerations
You need a thick rope or a long towel twisted up.

### Procedure
1. Put two actors on stage and have students in the audience define character, conflict, and setting.
2. The two characters proceed to improv their assigned scene with dialogue and one additional requirement: They each hold on to one end of a rope or towel, tug of war style.
3. They proceed through the scene, tugging on their end of the rope each time they try to move the conflict to their advantage.
4. Usually in a successful scene, the rope moves back and forth evenly, and each tug reveals deeper information about the situation.

   Coachings can include:

   Both characters remain physically and vocally active.
   Don't get stuck in repetitive arguments.
   Move the action forward.
   Embellish scene with detail.
   Reveal personal stories and histories.

5. Once students become successful with this technique, have them try the exercise with characters from scenes they are rehearsing.

## DIVIDED LINES

### Description
In this activity, the delivery of a single line becomes a collective responsibility. It is a helpful process for students who are memorizing lines from a script.
1. Have students get into pairs.
2. Assign each pair of students a neutral topic.

   | | |
   |---|---|
   | chores | the weather |
   | the kitchen sink | a newspaper |
   | a rug | the chicken pox |

3. Ask each pair of students to imagine and write down a lively sentence at least fifteen words long that relates to their topic:

Sometimes I get so tired doing chores around my house that I go to my room and listen to music.

4. Pairs must perform the sentence together, switching off every other word.

PARTNER A: Sometimes
PARTNER B: I
PARTNER A: get
PARTNER B: so
PARTNER A: tired

5. Coach students to avoid monotone, singsong, repetitive patterns.

Try to keep the natural rhythm of the words.
Don't let too much time lapse between words.
Don't anticipate words.
Use a student from outside of your pair to perform the sentence so you can duplicate the delivery.

6. After all pairs have delivered their sentence, bring the entire group together in a circle and assign a sentence with as many words as students. Rehearse, with each student performing one word.

# CHAPTER FIVE

# Performing

## FIELD NOTE EXCERPT: JENNIFER'S CLASSROOM

*Defining Performance*

*Right Before the Performance*

The backstage lights illuminate thirty ninth graders dressed in black pants and white T-shirts under a pale green glow. The thick curtains across the front of the stage form a visual barrier between the performers and their audience, but allow the murmur of the crowd and occasional voices of family and friends to float through. At the five-minutes-to-curtain cue, students move quietly into their opening positions.

As they move into place, the students give the appearance of being closer than they are in class—waving good luck to one another, squeezing hands, or grabbing impulsive hugs. Others no longer acknowledge those around them, moving into the concentration they will need throughout the show. Nervous limbs settle, silly giggling stifles, breathing deepens; the performers freeze, focus, wait.

Nahid, Celia, and Oriana stand next to the center opening in the curtains. They have volunteered to go out with me and provide the demonstrations to go with my preplay lecture.

"We're ready. I know we are," Nahid whispers.

"I heard my mom out there," Celia whispers.

"It's possible that I could throw up," Oriana whispers.

In the cycle of creative drama education, performance is reason for beginning and reason for ending; it is start-up and destination; it is test and reward. It is the ultimate chance to escape into other times and places, and it is also the time to stand up and be completely present. It is a place to feel both the pressure and the satisfaction of making personal efforts public. As my students ready themselves for their year-end

*Before I never had a goal; I never really liked to do anything. I was scared. When I found acting, I found a whole other world beyond mine. So every time before I perform, I just think about what I used to be, and what I am now today, and it instills confidence in me. To know that I can do this, I've overcome my obstacles.*

Nick, advanced acting student

play in the preceding field note passage, they demonstrate how the paradoxes of performance combine to create an intensely charged environment that, because it risks failure, breeds success.

Celia frames the performance for herself as a way to communicate with her mother in the audience. She hears her voice through the stage curtain and she no doubt thinks ahead to her introductory line in the play when she invites the audience to enjoy the play in Spanish, her mother's primary language. Celia later leads the whole cast in a brief wave and thank you to their mothers at the end of the play. For Nahid, the performance is the end of a long creating and rehearsal process. She calms her own nerves by reminding herself of how many times she has rehearsed the very same thing she will perform one more time tonight. For Oriana, the play is the beginning of a whole new experience, one that feels unlike anything we ever did in class, where she never once felt the kind of nervousness she feels now. But even with the overwhelming emotions that come with performance, she is able to call on her senses of humor and discipline.

There is a substantial difference between asking that something be learned or memorized and asking that something be performed; our last chapter explores this difference. In a school setting, students are often asked to "perform" on tests or written projects for an "audience" of one—the teacher. Not only is the teacher a very narrow audience, but she is far removed from each student performance. Papers are written at home, turned in during class, taken away, and returned later with written comments or a silent grade.

A commitment to using performance with youth is a commitment to include important aspects of learning that are too often put off until the last minute of a lesson or left out altogether:

reflection
self-evaluation
community connection
publication
saying thank you

Teachers recognize the importance of these abilities, but because they necessarily take place at the end of something, they stand in prime position to be given short shrift. And while teachers know that students who look back over work with a critical eye and include family and friends in the process do better than students who do not, the position of these abilities outside of specific curricula leaves them with a slippery reputation. Designing a project or lesson for youth with a performance at the center gives adults an opportunity and a method for offering these skills of success to every child involved.

In exchange for its insistence on performance, this chapter offers a widely flexible definition of what it means to perform with youth. Most basically, performance in this book means presenting something that has been rehearsed to a group of others for the purpose of engaging them. Using this definition, performance can involve

- a group of young people who read their own poetry at a senior citizen luncheon
- teenagers who bring a collection of theatre games to play with a group of elementary school children
- a class that invites parents in for breakfast to watch what goes on
- the student who has to perform his monologue to his family around the dining room table

Traditional requirements of performing scripted royalty plays—costumes, props, sets, lighting, makeup—demand so much money and technical expertise that they can shift the emphasis of an arts program from youth-centered to adult-centered. These traditional requirements can be downplayed and replaced with careful choices about what material to perform, for whom, and where—all choices youth can make and execute themselves. In the play my students were preparing, costumes were taken care of with black pants from the students' own wardrobes and a T-shirt with the silk-screened logo of their play. The same logo also decorated the program and flyers advertising the production. The stage for their play was set with shapes the students formed with their bodies rather than with constructed sets.

We used folding chairs and a single boxful of props—a simplicity that made it easy for us to rehearse and perform in different places. Much more will be said throughout this essay about performance venues, but what is important to note here is that definition of performance should not frighten us away from using it, but rather invite us to enjoy its unique benefits.

Consider the following poster defining the concept of performing.

*You Are PERFORMING Well When You:*

- Maintain Mental and Physical Fitness
- Balance the Emotions of the Ego with the Greater Goals of Performance

- Exhibit Flexibility and Resourcefulness
- Respect the Established Code of Performance
- Engage in Reflection

We tell adolescents to eat right, and get plenty of rest, and they will not do well at something if they are feeling poorly, but the demands of performance illustrate the point much more rigorously. The student who loses her voice cannot be heard by an audience, the student who is sick cannot muster the energy to perform, and a performance deadline is rarely a flexible thing that can be put off to accommodate someone's ill health. Part of performance's power comes from the fact that it requires players to choose, arrange for, publicize, and work toward a date. Each person is needed at show time and cannot be replaced.

As students realize their group effort needs them, they also know that no one individual can truly replace another. While lessons of the ensemble come together in the crucible of performance, each ego receives considerable attention during the performance process:

- undivided audience attention
- laughter
- silence
- empathy
- applause and cheers
- feelings of euphoria following the rush of performance adrenaline

These kinds of attention carry with them an addictive charge.

In creative ensemble theatre, however, individuals overly concerned with seeking personal gratification thwart the larger aims of the performance. They upstage ensemble members and knock the piece off balance, leaving the audience wondering how to react. Adolescence is a time of emotional experimentation and extremes. The performance space values emotion—in its actors and its audience—but provides clear boundaries for it. The actor lost in the sadness of his character or the euphoria of attention can no longer make the many choices performance demands.

Performance also offers a healthy high to adolescents. The high is created by performance's inherent risk, a risk that is healthy because it is calculated and constructive. But it is a risk. Young performers see early in the rehearsal process all of the ways a performance can go awry—dropped lines, character breaks, missed cues, technical mishaps, memory locks—all break the magic fourth wall and reveal a flawed piece to the audience. Students get nervous anticipating failure before a performance; this nervousness fuels the adrenaline rush that later contributes to their relief and pleasure at the conclusion of the performance. Successful performers see this nervous tension as part of performance, even as a sign that they are properly concerned with the task ahead, but they do not let it consume them.

Live performance makes it impossible to guarantee how events will proceed, so a clear head is essential to make decisions, compensate, flash forward and backward in sequence, cover for others, and accommodate audience reactions. No director can rush onstage to tell a performer what to do when a prop breaks or an actor skips an important cue, nor can she control how an audience will respond once a show has begun. Young performers start on their own, and this realization fuels their preperformance nervousness as well. They must rely on the lessons learned in rehearsal, their stagemates, and their own judgment. When this whole process works, and the many pitfalls are avoided or gracefully bridged, the feeling of accomplishment is significant.

One defining feature of creative drama groups—the postperformance discussion, in which the ensemble remains on stage after the curtain call to interact with the audience—formalizes the reflection process. Audience questions and comments come while the performance is still fresh in everyone's mind, but also provide the distance of perspective, because they ask students to see the performance from different perspectives.

Performing introduces participants to an established code of performance. This code, rather than being a hard and fast list of rules, is a collection of tenets guiding performers across the arts as they present their work to others. For example:

• Performers are expected to make themselves fully visible and audible to their audience, to create a performance in which the audience members do not have to exert undo effort while watching the performance.

• Performers are expected to refrain from upstaging their cohorts, to not stretch individual roles for the sole purpose of getting further attention at the expense of another.

• Performers are expected to respect the technical aspects of their craft—to treat their stage space well, replace props and costumes to designated places, and provide technical crews with the cues and cooperation they need to perform their jobs.

• Performers are expected to honor agreements forged in rehearsal, to remain faithful to the messages accepted at the beginning of a creative process, and not use an ensemble effort to push personal beliefs without prior discussion.

• Performers are expected to accept that audiences are entitled to form their own opinions about the work performed and even to discuss these opinions in a public forum, as the performance was delivered in the same.

Students begin to see that they are participating in something larger than their single effort, that they are entering into an artistic conversation that began before they entered and will continue long after they exit.

Following is an excerpt from my field notes that shows Jan using performance as a teaching technique in her class. Here students struggle to balance issues of the individual ego with those of the ensemble, are flexible and resourceful, attempt to adhere to the code of performance, and take time to reflect on what they have accomplished.

## FIELD NOTE EXCERPT: JAN'S CLASSROOM

### Recycle Your Mind

#### The Idea for the Performance

When Jan questioned students about lackluster attitudes one day, they reminded her that report cards had been distributed and many of them were unhappy with the marks they had earned. Their statements led into a conversation about high school and public education that lasted all period, at the end of which Jan asked students to write down their most vivid memories and opinions about education. Later that afternoon, Jan read through their writings carefully, highlighting stories and statements that struck her as strong or unique.

These excerpts became the basis of a collage students improvised and expanded into a one-act play. In it, after each student performs his or her individual piece, the play moves to a church revival scene in which a popular student from advanced acting class, Ray, is guest cast as the preacher. Ray's character leads a rousing service preaching what the class has agreed on as necessary elements for a sound education. The play closes with Ray leading the congregation-cast in a rhythmic chant that centers on the play title, "Recycle Your Mind."

#### Rehearsing the Performance

Recycle Your Mind is scheduled to be performed in the auditorium during the school day with three other classes' short plays for audiences of their peers and teachers. The students are beginning to get nervous about what it will mean to speak their minds openly about school *in* school and in front of those who run the school. This nervousness dissolves productive debates into bickering and dilutes the original power of the piece. When Ray comes to rehearsal one week before the all-school show, he is quickly frustrated by his inability to rouse the energy necessary to carry the revival scene.

### Setting the Performance

Jan takes in the situation as she watches this rehearsal. Later she told me that she was well aware of how the beginning students looked up to the energetic and talented Ray, and she was trying to decide on the spot if his words of criticism were going to depress the cast even more or inspire them to make the show work.

*When we took our play out to this rural school, the people there didn't really know what it was like for us growing up in the city. The way someone put it was, "We got a bucket of laughs and a bucket of tears." I mean, some people found funny things in it and were laughing, and other people saw sad things in it and were crying. To see people responding on that emotional level is what we strive for in this class: to connect with people on an emotional level.*

*Jodi, advanced acting student*

"Let's set up a performance for you tomorrow in class so that you can begin to take on that experience for yourselves," Jan suggests unexpectedly.

"What? Tomorrow?"

"Not too many people. I think Ms. Mackbee (the principal) would like to hear your feelings about education. She's been asking me if she can stop by with a photographer from the paper, because here they're doing an article this week. Mychael Rambo will be here tomorrow to work with advanced; maybe he can come early and watch you, too. Kim will be here. And Jennifer will be here; she teaches drama in California."

"But the performance isn't until next week," one young man insists.

"No," Ray counters, "the performance is whenever anybody's watching."

### Warming Up for the Performance

The next day when the students come into class the fluorescent lights are off and the theatre lights are turned on. The various chairs, theater blocks, and boxes of papers that normally litter the room are moved off to the side, and soft instrumental music is playing on the boombox. Adults and advanced acting students stand to the side of the performance space talking with one another, and the beginning acting students realize that Jan has been serious.

As the warm-ups draw to a close, the audience members stop talking, look for chairs, and get set to watch the show. Mary Mackbee, the principal, comes in halfway through the warm-ups with the photographer from the paper, who begins to move about the space and take pictures immediately upon entering. By the time the beginning acting students are standing in their warm-up circle holding hands and sending energy pulses from person to person, it is as though their performance has already begun. The atmosphere in the room is serious, quiet, and expectant.

### The Performance Itself

During a performance the actors must remain in character even when they are not speaking or moving. In rehearsal, Jan has had the students practice "stare-downs" for which students partner up and stare one another dead in the eye without laughing or showing any expression for prolonged periods of time. Now the students must transfer this skill to the stage and avoid the temptations to fidget, talk to neighbors, make eye contact with a friend in the audience, or stare at the ceiling. Their direction is to stand attentively and silently in the semicircle concentrating on the play.

One young woman who has built a reputation for dramatically cracking up during the stare-down exercises and during rehearsal (in fact, the rest of the class would often wait for her to lose it so that they could take a break and laugh with her) begins to experience some lip quavering and shoulder shaking, telltale signs. But the atmosphere during this performance is not the same as in class. No one is looking at her with hopeful expectation of a distraction. In fact, a boy who stands across from her scowls and gives a tiny shake of his head. The girl clenches her jaw, takes a deep breath, and rides out the urge to laugh.

In addition to listening to themselves and one another to get their cues right, the actors now have to listen to the audience for the first time. Jamellah's monologue about an elementary school teacher who brought in homemade pies for a fractions lesson brings laughter from the audience— laughter for which Jamellah has to pause. And while this laughter throws the whole ensemble for a bit of a loop, it energizes them as well. With this connection, the actors pick up the pace of the show, turn up the volume of their voices, and put additional dramatic risk into their lines.

One young man warned in rehearsal about rushing his lines steps out of the semicircle and rushes through his first five words, then seems to remember to slow down and stops completely. He turns the stop into a dramatic pause, maintains level eye contact with the audience and continues talking at a slower pace. Jan nods approvingly. Her lessons seem to have kicked in. In fact, he likes the dramatic pause technique so much that he repeats it.

As the play progresses, the students find their stage legs. The students who deliver angry lines about education do so with tight muscles, clipped words, and loud voices; the students who have proud memories of school stand with confident postures, open faces, and upbeat voice rhythms. The result is a lively listening experience for the audience who cannot readily predict which speaker will step from the circle next. When the revival scene breaks open at the end of the play, the audience can relax to take it all in. Ray, as the preacher, shouts out questions to his parishioners, who answer him in unison.

Chanting "Re-Cycle Your Mind, Re-Cycle Your Mind," the students on stage seem freed by the fact that they no longer have to speak by themselves. They eagerly throw themselves into unison lines. The energy is contagious and soon the audience is clapping and reciting with the cast. Ray's willingness and ability to transform himself into another character models a new level of commitment for the beginning acting students. As Ray's deep bass voice mimics a preacher with conviction, the beginning acting students become half actors–half audience, losing themselves in the illusion that they are in the midst of a holy-roller revival while, at the same time, furthering that same illusion with their own actions and words.

### After the Performance

This is a savvy audience for which to perform. While it is small—a total of six adults and four advanced acting students—each person brings experience with either performing arts or education to the gathering. The applause they provide at the close of the show is warm.

"Wait," Jan instructs. "This is your chance to get some feedback from your audience."

The students sit in a loose version of the semicircle they performed in and wait for audience members to raise their hands. Jan stands off to the side and emcees the comments. She calls on one advanced acting student who is struggling to attend classes.

"I liked the way you weren't afraid to get angry about the way this school has treated you. Like when you told your story about when that teacher just sent you out of the room, day after day. That wasn't even right."

There is a slightly uncomfortable pause in the room.

"Ms. Mackbee," Jan calls on the principal.

"Your play gave me a lot to think about. One of the things I thought about is why you are willing to express your ideas about education in this play, and why you don't feel comfortable doing the same thing in your classes. I need to think about this issue some more until we come up with some answers. I'm also glad you included positive stories here; I loved hearing about your teacher who baked those pies for your math class."

"I'd like to say that you all got it way more together today than yesterday. I could feel it," Ray offered.

"Yes. Today you rose to the challenge Ray issued you yesterday," Jan praised. "You were willing to follow his lead and match the excitement he brought to the piece. Now, what would happen if you didn't wait for Ray, if you brought your own excitement to the piece? I think now would be a good time to thank your audience for coming."

The evaluative scales in the following poster provide another means of reflection on performance. As with the evaluative scales offered in previous chapters, this poster encourages a balance between abilities at once linked on a single spectrum and separated at its polar ends.

Performance Evaluation Scales

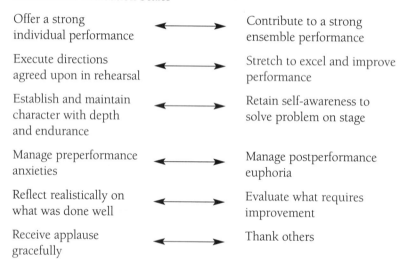

| | |
|---|---|
| Offer a strong individual performance | Contribute to a strong ensemble performance |
| Execute directions agreed upon in rehearsal | Stretch to excel and improve performance |
| Establish and maintain character with depth and endurance | Retain self-awareness to solve problem on stage |
| Manage preperformance anxieties | Manage postperformance euphoria |
| Reflect realistically on what was done well | Evaluate what requires improvement |
| Receive applause gracefully | Thank others |

## Teaching Performing

One glance reveals that the "exercises" in this chapter are different from those in other chapters. Much of what is offered here is a collection of guidelines and considerations that can be mixed and matched to design a performance experience. In my years of observing creative drama groups, I have seen a wide variety of performance scenarios, ranging from informal to formal.

## FIELD NOTE COLLECTIONS

### Performance Possibilities

#### Church Performance

A small, all-girl teen youth group performs before a church congregation during the Sunday service. The girls perform on the altar and the congregation watches from the pews for the fifteen-minute performance.

#### Teaching Teachers Performance

A collection of four different inner-city youth groups gather on a local college campus, each to perform a brief piece about learning for a group of professors of education and their students. At the end of the four ten-minute performances, all of the students come to the stage and take questions from the audience about their views on education and how they created their plays.

#### Rural and City High School Exchange

In an exchange between an inner-city drama class and a rural high school drama class, each shows the other a slide show with original narration about their own school. At the end of the slide shows, the two classes sit and talk in small groups over popcorn about the differences and similarities between their schools.

#### Summer Jobs Art Program

A group of eight high school students participate in a summer jobs program that pays them minimum wage to create, rehearse, and perform original one-act plays. They then tour to city recreation programs for elementary school students, performing in multiuse rooms and in parks. During the curtain call portion of each performance, actors go out into the audience and bring young children up on "stage" to sing and dance to the final musical number.

#### Police Performance

A group of "peace officers" training in neighborhood policing strategies visit a high school drama class, bringing with them improvisation situations they have collected from on-the-job interactions with teenagers. The drama students and their teacher then lead improvisation exercises in which the students and police take turns playing themselves and each other.

### On-the-Job Training

A group from a high school drama class travels to a local corporation head-quarters to present scenes showing how to best train a teenage worker. After the show is over, students call the adults "onstage" to replay situations from their piece with alternative problems and endings.

### College Preparation

A group of thirty students chosen for an Upward Bound college preparatory program (whose goal is to get at-risk students from high school to college) perform a play about their first year of academic high school for their families and teachers. Parents and teachers bring cookies; after the show students come down from the stage to talk to their audience.

### Social Work

A group of ten advanced acting students and their teacher travel to the local college to demonstrate for a class of youth work students how to use drama exercises as a learning tool. At the end of the performance workshop, the adult students are assigned to design their own uses for the exercises, appropriate for the specific populations with which they work.

### Special Education

A special education class invites a beginning drama class to their Kwanzaa party and asks them to bring acting exercises they can do together that illustrate the principles of the African-American holiday: unity, self-determination, creativity, and so forth.

### Story Hour

A group of ten teenagers pick their favorite children's stories, practice reading them, and then read them dramatically for story hour at the local day care center.

### Across the Curriculum

A history class joins up with a drama class to study local heroes and then create performances about them. Their joint performance at the end of their study satisfies requirements for each of their classes and honors the local heroes about whom they have written.

Jan and I have discussed many times in our collaboration our mutual ambivalence about grading in the drama classroom. On the one hand, the act of grading seems to have a forced place in theatre and the artistic process; on the other hand, assigning grades to students is a contractual obligation of teaching. Furthermore, the work students do in a well-run theatre class is significant and deserving of credit, and in school, credit is, literally, grades.

*The last two years have been really hard for Noel. So this has been a kind of anchor for him. When we went to the performance the other night, just to see all these kids and know something about some of their stories, and to see them all there on a Saturday night doing something positive was so hopeful.*

*Mother of intermediate acting student*

For me the grading debate is felt especially keenly because of my involvement in a special school-within-a-school college preparation program called 3-1-3. The program is a result of a collaboration between our school district and the local state college, which was looking to broaden its student base. It identifies students at the eighth-grade level who are motivated to attend college but at risk for rejection or dropout. All students are first-generation college attendees. Many represent ethnic groups the college campus would like to reach more often. The program's name is a formula for its purpose: If students pass their classes with acceptable grades, students will spend three years in high school, one year of combined high school and college instruction, and three years of college instruction. They end this sequence of years with a high school diploma and a college degree.

Program designers decided that all incoming ninth graders would take drama as a requirement rather than as an elective; they expect drama to teach the creative process and the ability to present oneself with confidence, as well as an additional shot of language arts studies.

While the creative aspects of this drama instruction are valued by the 3-1-3 program, grades are still a crucial part of the picture. To honor the goal of college preparation, I want to emphasize evaluation while still honoring performance as the final test of an actor's readiness. One technique to implement was the introduction of a point sheet in my drama class. With this method, students record their own grades, listing each assignment in the order that it was submitted, along with how many points it was worth and how many points were earned. Using this method, a student can average his or her grade at any time by dividing the number of points earned by the number of points possible. Students always know what grade they are earning, and they always know why they are earning it. The sample point sheet below was easily formatted with a table function on the computer.

| ASSIGNMENTS | POINTS POSSIBLE | POINTS EARNED |
|---|---|---|
| 1. Notes for Partner Interviews | 25 | |
| 2. Partner Interview Performances | 50 | |
| 3. Chart Five Influential Life Events | 25 | |
| 4. Improvisation Contest | 25 | |
| 5. Monologue Rough Draft | 25 | |
| 6. Monologue Response Sheet | 25 | |
| 7. Monologue Final Draft | 100 | |
| 8. Monologue Memorization Drill | 50 | |
| 9. Monologue Guest Director Sheet | 25 | |
| 10. Monologue Prop Check | 25 | |
| 11. Monologue Performance | 100 | |
| 12. Monologue Performance Comment Sheet | 25 | |
| 13. Weekly Reflections | 25 | |
| 14. Warm-up Performance Exam | 50 | |
| 15. Parts of Stage Quiz | 25 | |

I show students the categories I have created for my computerized grading program:

| | |
|---|---|
| quizzes | rough drafts |
| acting exercises | citizenship |
| reflections | family homework |
| organization | performances |
| written projects | memorization |

I also ask students the following questions about their grades:

- How do the assignments fit into the five stages of dramatic creation?
- Which categories reveal the best grades? the poorest?
- Which categories are worth the most?
- Which assignments do we have the most of?

Using a point sheet emphasizes evaluation and reflection and transfers much of the responsibility for an earned grade from teacher to student. Teenagers know that this responsibility belongs with them and are eager to take it, as long as they know how to do so.

One year my 3-1-3 drama students were gigglers. They saw each exercise as a new opportunity to get silly, and my asking or telling them to stop only made the urge to break character stronger. One day while leading warm-ups, I became frustrated to hear my own voice repeating the same nagging instructions—"Close your eyes for the meditation"— as I looked around to see numerous eyes popping open, or "Silence, please" as an anonymous somebody made a burping sound as we stretched.

The warm-up routine I use is a simple one that can be learned in a week or less; why were my students still dependent on me for instruction two months into the class? Or was I dependent on giving it to them? I thought of performance, and tried to merge elements of performance into a graded exam situation. The next day I walked into class, left a note for the students on a chair in the middle of the room, and departed. The note was entitled "A New Kind of Exam."

## CLASSROOM ASSIGNMENT: JENNIFER'S CLASSROOM

### The Performance Exam

*A New Kind of Exam*
- Today you will be taking an exam—a performance exam.
- You will be tested on how well you can lead yourselves through a set of warm-ups.
- You will have twenty minutes to rehearse as an ensemble while I am working next door.
- When I return to the room, I will expect to see a perfectly executed set of warm-ups, as well as a written outline on the board of what exercises you will be doing in what order.
- I will grade you on how well you follow the warm-up guidelines I have given you over the past two months.
- Your performance exam will be worth a performance grade of 50 points, which you will share as a class.
- Please respect our neighbors, and be no louder than if I were in the room with you. If I have to enter to ask you to be quiet, points will be deducted from your grade.
- Good luck.

From the inner work room where I now sat I could hear students quickly choose someone to read the instructions, someone to take notes on the board, and someone to keep an eye on the clock. They debated about which exercises to include, in what order, and what rules to follow. There were several audible, rather harsh directives ("Shut up!" "This is the way to do it!"), but almost all of these were followed quickly by a firm "Shhh!" and a reminder about time running out.

When I reentered the room, students stood dead quiet in a circle in the middle of the room. They had written a brief schedule on the board, revealing more organization than I had required and the kind of thoughtfulness I had hoped for. I stood watching the students in silence for thirty seconds or so, both to test their concentration and to enjoy the moment and then told them that they could start whenever they were ready. I circulated around the room as they performed, taking notes on a pad of paper. I vacillated between being impressed and a little peeved that they could do so well without me. Why should they do better without a teacher than with one?

---

One of the reasons this class was so silly in class was that I was not giving them enough responsibility for their own learning and success. They started out by acting silly, I reacted by clamping down, and they reacted by trying to subvert my new authority with more silliness, which made me tell them again to stop it. The use of performance in this exam allowed the students to become responsible for their own behavior, and left me functioning as a lesson designer and evaluator rather than as a disciplinarian.

A performance exam is a condensed performance experience: The rehearsal takes place in less than a class period, as does the performance; creativity is limited to the confines of what is being tested; and the audience, in this case, was limited to one person, the teacher. It works in large part because it mimics the larger, "real" performance experience, the culmination of extensive creation and rehearsal and a presentation to a formally assembled audience. As the chart earlier in this chapter reveals, performance is in no way limited to the traditional arena of the stage.

---

## FIELD NOTE EXCERPT: COLLEEN'S PREPERFORMANCE

### Observing Performance

One night in St. Paul Jan invited me to attended a high school dance concert directed by Jan's friend Colleen. I knew from previous conversations that Colleen had a special interest in the role of evaluation within the arts, and I was interested to see how this interest would manifest itself in the evening's performance.

When the lights went down in the theatre, which was large and full of parents, relatives, and students, Colleen came out onto the blank stage and stood in a spotlight. She welcomed the audience, thanked them for coming, and said she wanted to share with them some of the things the students in her classes had been learning. Colleen then named and briefly described five elements of shape in dance composition, calling different students onto the stage by name to demonstrate each element as she spoke.

"I'm going to call Shanice and Briana onto the stage now to demonstrate what counterbalance looks like in a dance." Then Colleen would prompt as the two girls hustled onto the stage and moved into a position where one was pushing against the other. Colleen walked briefly around the two girls, pointing out a few aspects of their position. The entire demonstration took no more than five minutes.

"Now you can watch for these elements as you enjoy our dances this evening," Colleen concluded. The audience was attentive during Colleen's talk; I certainly was, since I have had little formal dance training and was learning for the first time what she and her students were demonstrating.

On the way home from the concert, Jan and I discussed the simple effectiveness of Colleen's introduction:

- It educated the audience rather than simplified the performance.
- It elevated the level of responsibility for students who were performing.
- It transferred evaluation responsibility from teacher to audience.
- It legitimatized the good learning and teaching done by Colleen and her students.

Throughout our years of conversation after this dance concert, Jan and I have collected the different methods we have developed of educating our audiences before performances.

## FIELD OBSERVATION COLLECTION

### Ways to Begin a Performance

#### Making Warm-ups Public

If an ensemble regularly engages in a warm-up routine, the familiarity of this routine can have a calming effect on actors prior to a performance. In addition, watching how an ensemble warms up its body, voice, and concentration demonstrates for the audience the strenuous nature of performance.

### Distributing the Script

I have done this for plays cast with students in the process of learning English as a second language, students with hearing difficulties or speech impediments, or very new performers shy to the idea of projecting themselves. Rather than allowing the actors to slack off, this device holds actors more accountable because audience members can follow along and detect any mistakes made. Audiences are always impressed to see a nicely printed script; the pages of writing reveal how much work the students have done to create the play. Scripts can also be passed out afterward as a memento.

### Distributing an Evaluation Form

In the exercise section of this chapter Jan lists types of evaluation forms that can be handed out to an audience after a show for feedback. When handed out before a performance begins, these forms offer an audience specific ways to focus on the play.

### Explaining Things to Look For

A director, actor, or combination thereof can simply come out onto the stage and explain what the play is about, what skills it demonstrates, or what the actors would like the audience to look for. This was Colleen's approach.

### Illustrating Things to Look For

Colleen also used this technique when she called individual students on stage to demonstrate the moves audience members were to look for during the dance performance. This method can also be implemented without the director, with actors alone coming onto stage with signs, a narrator, or choral announcements to punctuate the demonstrations.

### Showing Before and After

If the intent is to demonstrate specific principles that improve a performance, an effective demonstration can be fashioned by having actors give a brief performance without, and then with, the desired principle. For example, if students have been working on injecting risk into the performance to make it more compelling, students can deliver a few lines from the play first without, and then with, risk.

### Explaining the Process of Creation

Many if not all in the audience will be watching an original play for the first time. Outlining the steps followed to create the play provides the audience insight into the students' work and helps to prepare them for the differences between a traditional and a creative production. Directors or students can also write about this process in the play program.

### Preshow Reception

Hosting a preshow hors d'oeuvre, dessert, or beverage reception gives actors a chance to mingle with the audience before going onstage. In one-on-one or small-group conversations, actors can explain what they will be doing within the play, how the play was conceived, or even confide their concerns—all interesting points for audience members to follow as they watch the show.

Often after a performance, Jan asks her students to write her a letter about how the performance went for them. This chapter ends with a collection of letters written by a beginning acting class after they performed a collection of original scenes for a group of students at their own high school. The students had performed some controversial material that involved risks, and Jan was interested to know how these first-time actors had processed the experience. The day after their performance, once they had had time to hear one another's comments and think about their time onstage, Jan casually asked students to write their reactions.

Students scrounged around for paper, pencils, and pens and cleared out a place on the theatre floor to sit and write their notes. What they wrote reveals that:

- They have learned to speak in the language of performing arts.

- Jan's students represent a wide array of the learning spectrum: Some are very comfortable communicating in writing, others struggle to craft the language, but all appear to be comfortable talking to Jan.

- Performance produces a nervousness and euphoria that make a big impression on the participants.

- Adolescents are equally concerned about issues of ego and friends.

- The stages of the process—using a receptive mind, working as an ensemble, creating unique work, and rehearsing effectively—continue to surface even after the first performance takes place.

- Performance is a method of discovery—of what we like, what we do not like, and what we might be able to do if we try.

- Student actors perceive performance as a gift.

## POSTPERFORMANCE LETTERS: JAN'S CLASS

### Evaluating a Risky Performance

Dear Jan,

I really like the play. It felt good when the people jump in joy when I said my part. At first I was scared, because all of those people was looking on. But I say to myself, why am I scared? I am not a scared person. I need to think bolder.

Dear Jan,

I really liked being the "Comic Relief" for a very serious issue. I liked doing a play that was controversial. I want to learn more serious acting for myself. I thought it was really fun afterward, when a few of us stayed and talked to the school that came to watch us. Thanx.

Dear Jan,

I think my friends were really shocked that I did a play like that but I told them I like showing a different side of me so that they can see that I have a serious side about me. I would like you to help me get more into my character so I can feel more comfortable. Thanks a lot for everything. I feel you really opened my eyes more.

Dear Jan,

Well I feel that we didn't have enough time to do our play. Not saying that everybody didn't work hard, but I felt that we worked the hardest because we kept changing our scene. We were the last ones to go up and besides that we got cut off and that made me upset. So I'll say what we needed is to perform our scene in front of the class.

Jan,

I was really, really NERVOUS when I went up—I was shaking, but once I got past that fear of the audience completely kicking me off the stage, it felt good to have something to give—my message to share. I felt empowered, and I had this tremendous energy. I liked it that it was controversial. It is important to get people to think about things. Thanks.

# Performance Warm-ups

*Exercises for Managing Expectation and Exercises for Critique*

## REFLECTION

Reflection is an ongoing activity that deepens the learning experience and can be helpful before a performance. Lead students through a short visualization to bring the last performance into mind. Then begin a discussion focusing on what went well, what needs to be changed, what they are learning, or other issues students want to address. Reflection is a time to make connections and reinforce specific skills being taught.

## BRUSH-UP REHEARSAL

During the run of a show, focus on a scene that has gone stale or somehow lost its original luster. As a warm-up, have the whole group work on changing or improving a specific moment in the play. Help students view the performances as a process of rewriting and improving their work. Audience feedback and group evaluation offer helpful suggestions for change, while keeping the performance energy up and the quality of the work high.

*Exercises for Gratitude*

## DEDICATIONS

Dedications consist of students gathering together in a circle to dedicate their efforts to someone or something outside of themselves. Begin with a standing relaxation with a focus on breathing. Next, each person makes a dedication either silently or aloud. Close with a short activity to connect the ensemble, such a passing an impulse hand to hand.

## AWARDS

Assign each student a classmate for whom they will create a simple award. Provide art supplies and time in class to begin the project. Allow time before a performance for a ceremony where each student is acknowledged in front of the group and presented with the special award.

## OFFERINGS

Ask each student individually to come to the center of the circle with an offering to the group that shares how they hope to carry what they have learned into their own separates lives and communities. They can speak, sing, dance, move, or communicate in whatever form fits. Each student has a turn.

*Exercises for Concentration*

## LINE-THROUGH

In a line-through, students sit in a tight circle and simply run the lines in their play. All lines should be delivered in character; if a mistake is made they are to cover it and keep on going. Use a stopwatch and encourage speed and accuracy.

## PERFORMANCE VISUALIZATION

Immediately before a performance, take the students on a guided visualization of the performance. Begin by having them visualize themselves backstage before the show with the lights going down. Then talk them through scene by scene, having them focus on themselves, the group, costume changes, or any helpful component. This technique has been used for many years to improve athletes' performance.

## FIRST LINE, LAST LINE

As a quick warm-up, have students run a condensed version of the show, delivering only the first and last few lines of each scene. Focus instead on the entrances and exits, set changes, and transitions between scenes. This tightens the piece, refreshes the scene order, and helps actors adjust to different-sized stages while on tour.

## LETTERS

To help students relax into character before a show, have them close their eyes and imagine their character at a specific moment in the show. Instruct them to write a letter, in character, to someone they trust, such as a friend, a relative, God, or maybe just to themselves. Ask them to reveal something special in the letter and to write from their hearts. Let volunteers read their letters to the ensemble.

## ENDURANCE EXERCISE

Because performing demands physical endurance, it's helpful to integrate physical exercise into the preshow warm-up routine. Try running laps around the auditorium or performing space followed by an aerobic routine and stretches. Have students take turns preparing and leading the physical warm-up.

## VOCAL WORK

Tongue twisters, breathing exercises, and back rubs can help relax and ready students for the vocal demands of performance. Have the students stand in a straight line across the stage facing the audience seats. Have them practice throwing their voices to the back row. Have one student sit in a remote seat and coach actors for projection.

*Kids are cautious about saying they have solutions. But they do say that drama helps them, when something is going on at school, to go out and do theatre. We offer a way to get some kind of perspective so that young people can observe it and be on the outside making their heads look at the whole thing in a different way. Having fun is also key. After something hard happens, being able to watch something and kick back to get some space from it builds the spirit back up so they can go on.*

## INDIVIDUAL WARM-UP ROUTINES

Have students create their own preshow warm-up routine. Suggest an approximate length and specific elements to include such as physical, vocal, and concentration exercises. Set aside a specific time for students to work individually on their personal warm-up routine.

### Exercises for Maintaining Ensemble

## SURFACING TENSION

For subtle tensions affecting the unity of the ensemble, give each student a small file card and ask students to anonymously describe any problem or tension they have observed. Use the feedback to help you address the situation, or read the cards out loud and have the students react and suggest a solution. Anonymity is sometimes necessary in identifying and resolving group problems.

## PLAYGROUND TAG

As a quick preshow warm-up, have students choose partners. Person A is IT and chases Person B; then Person B is IT and chases Person A. Freeze after a few minutes and repeat with new partners.

## OBJECT TOSS-IN

Gather students into a circle. Toss in an object that can be thrown safely. Instruct students to throw the object around the circle until everyone has tossed the object to someone else one time only. Repeat the toss in the exact same pattern, making sure everyone knows to whom they throw the object and from whom they receive it. Once the object is moving smoothly on its course, toss in a second object, instructing the group to keep it moving along the same path as the first. As the group concentration improves, toss in more objects. Coach the group to stay silent while working.

## SOUND AND MOVEMENT UNIFY

Working in small groups of five or six, have each student begin his own repeatable sound and movement. Once each student has his own unique expression, call out "Unify!" The large group must then slowly transform all the individual sounds and movements into one unified piece.

## Exercises for Teaching Performance

### Creating A Performing Environment

Whether you perform in your classroom, in the gym, on a stage, or at another location on tour, you can transform the performing space into something bright and welcoming with minimal hassle and expense. Keep it simple.

#### Transforming the Space

Enlarge inspirational quotations reflecting the values of the program or poems and slogans written by students. Alternatively, use quotations from the play itself as displays. Laminate them and decorate the space. Let students take pictures of each other, and enlarge them or make photo collages illustrating the process of creating the work and hang them up. Fabric banners can be used for color and even written on if desired.

#### CallBoard

Identify a wall or a bulletin board that can be the "CallBoard" or communication center for the group. Post announcements, daily schedules, calendars, auditions, job opportunities, support services for youth, relevant news articles, and other information of interest to young people and their community.

#### A Portable Set

Basic elements such as ladders, wooden boxes, simple scaffolding, benches, chairs, risers, Styrofoam, and cardboard are easily portable and can create an effective performing space.

#### Seating

Arrange the performance space so that the audience is as close as possible to the performance area. The audience can sit on chairs, on the floor, or on carpet squares.

#### Costumes

A basic cast costume can be created by asking each student to wear a pair of blue jeans and a white T-shirt or, if possible, a T-shirt designed with the title of the play. Accent costume pieces such as hats, glasses, scarves, or gloves can be collected from cast participants and found at second-hand stores.

### Technical Needs

A boombox for music or sound effects is adequate; however, acquiring your own sound system with an amplifier, speakers, and microphones enhances the quality of the sound and creates more options for performance. If lighting is a desired effect, placing standard 65- or 75-watt light bulbs in #10 tin cans help create atmosphere.

## What To Perform

A process can be set up to help students select the best venue for their performances. Students will need to consider what they will perform, for whom they will perform, and what resources are available to them. Considerations might include

| | |
|---|---|
| time (to prepare and to perform) | financial resources |
| desired audience | ability level of students |
| goals for student learning | space considerations |
| community support | transportation |

Performance can take a variety of forms and may happen throughout the course or as a closing event. Performance can be as simple as teaching a sample class for an audience or as extensive as presenting a fully produced original play. Whatever the choice, as the pressure of performance creeps into the work process, it is important to remember not to lose sight of the purpose of the work and the educational needs of the students. Following are some suggestions for presenting work.

### A Collage of Short Scenes

Original scenes, stories, songs, and poems can be fashioned into a short play. They can be ordered for contrast and dramatic build. Transitions can be crafted to give a sense of unity to the piece.

### A Series of Monologues

Individual or shared monologues can be presented as a performance. Try placing the entire group on stage at once with individuals taking turns to perform.

### Polished Class Exercises

Class activities can be rehearsed, polished, and presented. Select a class exercise that lends itself to performance. For example:

| | |
|---|---|
| Rituals | Soundtrack |
| Living Newspapers | Creating Writing and Movement |
| Basket Scenes | Long-Distance Journeys |

### A Sample Class

Teach a sample class in front of an audience. Connect activities with a unifying theme. Or, use activities to demonstrate the teaching of specific skills. Good choices for activities include those that allow many or all students to rotate through the exercise, giving everyone a chance to contribute and be seen, such as:

| | |
|---|---|
| Scenes in Lines | Tag Out Scenes |
| Transformation Scenes | Car Play |
| Machines on Themes | Three and a Box |

### Staged Poetry

Generate original poetry. Create body sculptures and visual images to bring the poems to life. Individuals can read poems or groups can transform poems into vocal collages.

### Interactive Theatre with Audience

Here audience members become involved in the stage event. The audience can be invited

into the action on stage
to share stories that can be used as material for improvisation
to make suggestions about how to end a scene.

### The Beginning of a Play

Give students a chance to perform for a small or friendly audience while the play is still in the rehearsal process. This dress rehearsal provides an opportunity for audience feedback.

### Full Productions

Full productions accommodate entire original plays with a developed plot line or a connecting thematic presence throughout the work. They require extensive rehearsal and rigorous effort.

### Cold Readings/Staged Readings of Original Scripts

Students work individually on writing scripts. Have students sit on stage and read scripts in character. Or, block the scene and have students present the work with scripts in hand.

### Student Playwriting Festival

A playwriting festival can be the focus for an entire course. Begin with activities that inspire confidence in the written word. Focus on encouraging individual students to share stories through writing. Collect student work and stage informal readings. Allow time for rewriting. Consider pairing student writers with mentor artists during the rewriting process. Select writings to be produced. Choose experienced students or community artists to direct student work. Create a Play Festival Performance presenting the highlights of student work.

## Selecting an Audience

Students can identify who their audience will be based on the content of the performance, the collective goals of the group, and the resources of the program.

### An Arts Class or Compatible Group from Your School

This is a convenient and safe way to present or preview a performance. It can be as simple as a casual arrangement between two teachers. Small groups allow for more honest and attentive discussion afterwards. A class can visit more than once to witness the performances in different stages.

### Breakfast Theatre for Family Members

Students organize a simple breakfast and informal performance. Family members get involved in the process; parents can attend on their way to work. Local bakeries are often willing to make donations. This option provides an attentive audience and heightens the energy in the classroom.

### Kindergarten/Preschool

Preparing to perform for small children can be a fun and freeing process. This enables further exploration of animal characters, fables, fantasy, and masks.

## Elementary Schools

Small children can be receptive audiences and eager participants. They are willing to look up to the older students as role models. Scheduling is usually flexible in elementary schools.

## Junior High and High Schools

Performance can become a catalyst for dialogue with the audience. However, scheduling performances can be more difficult. Identify a teacher or a program willing to be a liaison with your group. Also contact a diversity group, performing arts program, youth service, or student council. Performances can help to support ongoing efforts in the sponsoring school.

*It's scary when I'm up there performing. Because I don't know how they're going to react. But I know it takes everyone's cooperation to make a piece. And when everyone is cooperating, you don't care what the audience thinks. Because you know inside how you feel, and you're just trying to get it out to the audience.*

*Mary, intermediate acting student*

## Alternative Youth Programs

These programs are a way to reach kids who for a variety of reasons are not succeeding in the public schools, as well as young people in shelters or with other special needs. These agencies are usually open to creating a relationship with a theatre program. Voices of youth in these programs are made more visible through arts workshops. The needs and sensitivities of both groups should be carefully matched. The arts can become a way to foster dialogue in settings that are often more intimate.

## Adopt a School

By planning with adopted schools, students can create theatre to interface with the school curriculum. It can become ongoing work with more regular visits. Student actors can even create theatre based on the written work of kids at the adopted school. Pen pals and peer helper relationships can be formed.

## Colleges/Professional Organizations

Adults who work with young people welcome student productions as part of training seminars and conferences. Performances offer an opportunity for adults to dialogue with young people. Performances also introduce adults to theatre methods to use with youth. It is valuable for the student performers to be treated with respect and viewed as specialists.

### Prisons/Incarcerated Youth

Prison performances offer a chance to share with and learn from a population that is often forgotten. Students performing need to be mature, socially conscious, and respectful. The material should be appropriate. The first step is to contact the recreation director or local organization that maintains an ongoing service relationship with inmates.

### Community Elders

Elders are a vast resource of knowledge. Theatre confronts stereotypes about age and forges new understanding. Seniors can watch or be involved in workshops. Identify organizations serving elders and invite them to a performance. Grandparents are an enthusiastic audience and can be invited to school and included in creating the show.

### Coalitions of Local Groups

Local organizations, neighborhood groups, city commissions, and business partnerships can work together to sponsor a theatre performance. This process builds a support base to sustain theatre work for youth. A larger support base helps get the voice of the kids heard in a larger arena by generating additional media coverage and publicity.

### Friends, Family, Neighborhood

Have the students invite their friends and family to an informal evening performance. Pass the word, copy some flyers, and hang some posters to publicize the event. Have everyone bring some food for a reception afterward.

### Additional Suggestions

Libraries, community centers, children's museums, state and local government are all possible audience venues.

## Publicizing for a Community Performance

Since an important part of this work is impacting the community and helping young people to make their voices heard, it is important to include publicity and program promotion in the process.

### Create a Strategy

Create a publicity strategy with the class or with a focus group of interested students. Encourage creativity and provide resources for students to reach their desired audience.

### Get the Word Out

Have students design and print posters, flyers, and invitations. Bring posters to strategic locations such as churches, local recreation centers, libraries, coffeehouses, special events, or anywhere they can get the word out to the people they want to reach.

### Identify Sponsors

Recruit a local business that can assist with publicity as a cosponsor or make a financial contribution in exchange for an ad in the program.

### Teach Students to Write a Press Release

Include who, what, when, where, and some quotations from the kids in the play. Create or borrow a press contact list and send press releases to all major and community newspapers and local television stations. Check with your local cable access channel to see if they will run a public service announcement. See Appendix Four for a sample press release.

### Make Follow-up Calls

Have students role-play conversations with press, radio, and television contacts. Then have them make the calls and work with the media to publicize their work.

### Involve Parents, Guardians, and Family Members

Involve family members in publicity, poster design, and ticket sales. Invite parents to perform or be the master of ceremonies at community events.

## Touring Responsibilities

Almost all aspects of taking a show on tour can be managed by students. Below is a breakdown of tour responsibilities.

## Booking

Identify contact names for booking the tour.
Create and mail out a booking letter. Follow up with a phone call.
Confirm tour dates and mail out contracts.
Design a list of special requests for the sponsoring school.
Identify a student group or sponsor whose mission the cast wishes to support.
Request juice and cookies for the cast and crew after the show.
Request technical assistance (lights and sound).
Send thank-you letters after the performance.

## Transportation

Make a list of set pieces to be carried by the school truck.
Maintain ongoing contact with set movers.
Double-check buses the day of tour.
Carry phone numbers for the bus company and furniture movers at all times.

## Communication

Create a system (such as a CallBoard or phone tree) to inform all cast members of the time, date, and place of shows.
Determine and execute a replacement system for sick or missing cast members.
On the day of tour, make sure everything and everyone is on the bus (check list).
Give bus driver the OK to leave.
Upon arrival, check in and get directions to the performing space.

## Pack-Out

Create a detailed pack-out list of everything to take on tour.
Work closely with the sound crew and prop and costume manager.
Take charge of pack-outs and clean-ups.

## Costumes and Props

Create a system to store and transport the costumes and props.
Get prop boxes and costumes ready for pack-out; make sure everything is there.

Work with stage managers to organize props and costumes backstage.
After shows, collect company belongings and store them back in boxes.
Repair or replace damaged costumes and properties.

### Stage Management

Locate bathrooms and dressing rooms; define space for personal belongings.
Find tables for props and costumes.
Arrange for water backstage.
Work with light and sound technicians at the sponsoring school.
Gather cast and explain show time and schedule.
Lead warm-ups.
Work with the sponsoring school to determine introductions.
Run the show from backstage, monitoring cues and unforeseen problems.

### Music and Tech

Carry all sound and music equipment in and out of the bus.
Set up the sound system.
Test all tapes, CDs, microphones, and sound levels.
Set up and take down scaffolding and boxes for the show.
Assist with clean-up.

> *Actors are responsible not to put stereotypes up on stage. You can't completely avoid that; sometimes they're done in humor. We always ask our audiences if we're putting any harmful stereotypes out there. We may not agree with them all the time, but we ask. Actors are responsible to be creating believable, honest characters.*

# Final Thoughts

As teacher-researchers we are most challenged by the question, "So what?" So we design a more effective way to teach a subject or structure a program or reach a group of students—how does that connect to the larger picture of improving the lives of youth?

This book is dedicated to detailing a method of performing arts education for adolescents. So what? For us, the answer is that involvement in the arts leads young people to healthier, more fulfilling lives. We believe this because of our own experiences with art and because of the kinds of observations we report in the pages of this book. In this conclusion we present a third kind of proof of the importance of involvement in the arts.

Since 1987 a team of researchers at Stanford University has been studying youth organizations in inner cities, economically depressed midsized towns, and rural areas in the United States. This team has sought to discover how youth groups serve their members successfully even when other institutions in their communities do not.

It was as a member of this research team, looking specifically at art-based youth groups, that the two of us met. The way in which Jennifer observed the youth of Central Touring Theater is representative of how the Stanford researchers involved themselves in the lives of youth group members and collected data about how they learn.

As part of this data collection, the research has asked youth group participants to complete the National Longitudinal Education Survey (NLES), which provides a national database of information based on 22,000 students from a representative sample of American high schools. This comparison between American youth in general and American youth who elect involvement in art-based youth groups allows us one more measure of the arts' positive effects.

In a sentence, this comparison shows that even though the youth who are drawn to membership in community art groups come from more difficult circumstances than others taking the NLES survey, they fare better in the results. The core finding of the comparisons are provided as the answers to four central thoughts.

**Who are the young people finding their way to art organizations?**

Compared to American youth in general, they have

more tumultuous home situations.
more violent school settings.
felt more direct effects of periods of economic downturn.
felt less safe in their schools and communities.

**What do they do?**

They have

won academic honors.
been recognized for school and community service.
received honors for their writing.
been elected school class officers.

**How do they feel about themselves?**

They feel sure they

will seek future education after high school.
can make plans they will accomplish.
are persons of worth.
are able to do things as well as others.

**In their futures, they feel it will be important to**

help others in their communities.
work to correct economic inequalities.
have a better life than their parents have had.

These findings provide strong backup as we face the "So what?" question as arts educators. Jan describes that the dramatic arts have provided her with a "path that fits both feet," so that she can walk as both artist and educator. This book is our claim that the art of drama forges a path to learning and change, both for those who walk it as teachers and for those who travel it as students.

# Sample Lesson Plans

The following sample lesson plans from Jan's classroom provide examples of how exercises can be sequenced over several days. Because interaction with students will always shape and reshape lessons, these are not offered as rigid guidelines. The process of teaching with these exercises requires teachers to follow their students' lead as they lead their students.

Most of the activities listed here are exercises already described within the chapters, which can be reread for a complete reference. Also provided here are brief summaries of exercises, recommendations on transitioning from one activity to the next, and mention of the skills addressed by each exercise.

## Opening Week

For me, the primary goal of the opening week is to assess the skill level of students, to get a sense of the group's personality and begin to create a safe working environment. Through these introductory activities, students get to know each other and learn what will be expected of them in class.

### Day 1: Take A Risk

*Chairplay*
Students sit in a circle of chairs, changing places frequently. This activity allows low-risk group interaction and introduces the class as a hands-on participation experience.

*Daily Sharing*
Have students remain in the circle.
The ritual of coming together and sharing is introduced as everyone says their name and answers a given question.

*Expectations*

Have students remain in the circle to introduce the concept of safe space.

Also introduce expectations, class philosophy, grading criteria, and ground rules.

*Groupings*

The class moves around the room, grouping and regrouping in different categories. This provides interactions with new people and an opportunity to learn names.

*The Predator and the Prey*

The group returns to the circle.

The "Predator" in the middle tries to tag the "Prey" with eyes closed.

The ensemble participates in complete silence, awakening senses and working as a team.

*Walk and Notice*

Instruct the group to walk around the space, observing the room and their classmates, then pausing to answer questions with their eyes closed.

*Listen and Repeat*

Transition into this exercise by having each student find and face a partner.

Students share stories and create connections by speaking, listening, and then repeating back what they hear.

*Impulse Pass*

Close the class by asking students to return to the circle.

Review skills and expectations.

Allow time for questions or feedback.

Hold hands and pass an impulse (hand squeeze) in total silence.

## Day 2: Building Ensemble

*Unity Circle*

Bring everyone into one circle.

Review ground rules.

Have students quickly split into two teams for tape ball.

### Tape Ball Toss

Each team gets one ball and begins counting the number of tosses.

Tape ball becomes a physical and vocal warm-up as well as a team builder.

Coach for cooperation.

### Walk and Freeze

Have students move around the room, being respectful of each other's space.

Teach the concept of the freeze by starting and stopping movement randomly.

Music adds energy and relieves tension.

### Changing Partner Warm-up

When students seem comfortable moving in the space, ask them to find a partner.

Students preview a variety of acting skills while working with a different person each time.

### Partner Interviews

The last partner in Random Walk becomes the introduction partner.

Give students ten minutes to interview each other and introduce partners to the class.

### Power Clap

If there is time, gather the group together in a circle.

Have students close their eyes and reflect upon the day.

Then begin the power clap exercise, striving for group focus and unity.

## Day 3: Creating Ensemble

### Sound and Movement Circle

Have students stand in a circle.

Ask students to create a sound and movement showing how they are feeling.

Rehearse simultaneously.

Share individually.

*Sound and Movement One-Two-Three*

Building on sound and movement expression, students work in partners in this challenging concentration exercise.

*Walk, Freeze, Find an Object*

Everyone moves around the room, stopping to create and explore imaginary objects with senses and emotions.

*Meal Mirrors*

Call students back into partners.
One partner creates a character and an activity.
The other partner mirrors.

*Basic Improv Scenes*

Two volunteers stand up.
Ask the class to define who they are, where they are, and to suggest a conflict.
Allow the two volunteers to begin the scene.
Freeze at a heightened moment and repeat the process.

## Day 4: Building Trust

*Object Toss In*

Tossing objects around the circle demands focus.
It also builds trust and reinforces ensemble spirit.

*Sculptures in Partners*

Creating and mirroring images introduces a powerful form of communication and expression.
Have students change partners several times to create and reflect shapes and emotions.

*Support Shapes*

Support Shapes requires some intimate connection and risk.
It can build ensemble and set a tone of cooperation.

*Discussion*

After the Support Shapes exercise is a good time to discuss the value of safe space and trust in the creative process.

### Day 5: Creating Scenes

*Body Part Tag*

Shift out of yesterday's intensity with a high-energy game of tag.
Reinforce the goal of becoming comfortable with physical contact.

*Directed Movement*

Build on movement expression.
Layer emotions, use of space, and slow motion onto movements.

*Soundtrack*

Working in small groups, students improvise silent scenes to music.
Coach for a clear beginning, middle, and end.
Allow a short time for rehearsal and then share scenes.

*Reflection*

Have students reflect on the week in writing or discussion.
For example, ask them to recall skills they have learned, risks they have taken, or important topics that have come up in the process.

## Creating Characters and Scenes

The following series of activities is designed to have students explore scene and character work. The primary purpose is to allow students to learn about themselves and each other, and then use to express what they have learned. Ideas for play topics and projects often evolve from this kind of daily work.

### Day 1: Introduction to Scene Work

*Ensemble Vocal Warm-up*

Students begin class in a circle divided into four sections.
As groups speak a single line together, they experience the power of the ensemble.
This warm-up is an equalizer; it shelters risk for the most shy and brings the most individualistic into the ensemble.

*Scene Starts in a Circle*

Students remain in the circle.
Each person recalls and shares a familiar phrase heard at home.

The ensemble immediately echoes the line back.
This reinforces the job of the group to support its members.

*Defining Who, What, and Where in Lines*

Begin with one student miming an object.
The second student joins the improv, defining the scene further
with a spoken line.
Everyone gets a short turn defining Who, What, and Where with
a partner.
The quick pace encourages spontaneity.

## Day 2: Basic Elements of a Scene

*Tug of War Warm-up*

This warm-up with an imaginary rope reestablishes group
energy.
It requires cooperation when actors try to make the rope look
real.
It requires conflict as each side's goal is to win the game.

*Scene Jump Starts in Threes*

Direct everyone to form groups of three, where each group
creates short scenes simultaneously.
Beginning and ending the scenes in a freeze relieves the anxiety
of where to start and stop the action.
This also creates a frozen and focused group of students
receptive to coaching and direction.

*Reflection*

Take time to reflect on what has been learned, felt, and
experienced.
Support creative choices and acknowledge risk.
Refer back to the goals and philosophy of the work.
Encourage discussion about issues important to students and
their communities.

## Day 3: The Body as a Resource for Character

*Personality Tag*

IT creates an individual character walk.
Others in the group recreate the same walk as they move around
the room playing tag.

Call out "Freeze" during the tag game and coach students to create characters based on specific walks.

### Characters from the Freeze

Have students walk, run, skip, and then freeze.
Alternatively, call out an emotion and have students create that emotion physically, then freeze.
Encourage students to let a character emerge from the shape of their bodies.
Then bring the character to life by directing an activity or by coaching the characters to whisper thoughts out loud.
Have students share character choices with each other.

### Character Environments

Have students initiate new characters by shaping and reshaping their bodies.
Suggest an environment such as a bus depot, a family picnic, a child care center.
Have students transform the space by creating characters and action with pantomimed objects.
Coach characters to begin their actions in silence, then transition into gibberish or words.
Encourage character interaction.
Use the "Freeze" command to listen to a small grouping of characters or introduce a common event that everyone can respond to.

### Internal Character Voice

Have students close their eyes and remember the characters they created this day.
Ask them to select their favorite and write out that character's thoughts.
Students can partner up and read their work to each other.

## Day 4: A Serious Focus

### Group Meditation

Gather students into a circle.
Have them inhale and exhale together ten times silently and sit down.

### Making Connections

Ask for two volunteers to sit face-to-face in the middle of the circle.

The challenge is for everyone to concentrate deeply enough so that the two in the middle can say to each other "I want you, I need you, I love you" sincerely, without laughing.

*Serious Moment*

Have students partner up and create a sixty-second scene that reveals a serious interaction.
Limit rehearsal time to ten minutes.
Scenes can end with a resolution or freeze at a heightened moment.

*Scene Sharing*

Have students return to the circle.
Students can perform their partner pieces in the center of the circle.
Coach for consistent focus, good listening, and believable emotion.
Remind the group that the ensemble is responsible for maintaining an environment that supports risk and creativity.

## Day 5: Relaxation and Recall

*Count to Twenty*

Divide the class into groups of eight to ten.
Have each group form a tight circle and close eyes.
As a group, but without any kind of leader or signals, students must try to count to twenty with only one person saying each number.
For example, if two people say "three" at the same time, the group must start again.
They must start over again until they can count straight to twenty with only one person saying each number.

*Meditation*

Turn down the lights, if possible.
Ask students to lie down or just get comfortable in a chair.
Play some relaxing music and take them on a memory journey into their past.
For example, remember specific years in junior high or elementary school.
Afterward give students ample time to write, reflect, and share their feelings.

*Reflection*

If the session has been emotionally demanding, remember to
provide closure, such as

| | |
|---|---|
| group dancing | sharing circle |
| group scream | a quick game of freeze tag |

## Day 6: Small-Group Scene Work

*Choosing a Topic*

Have students form new small groups.
This time have students talk about and list topics or themes
important to them and select one to work with.

*Sculpting an Image*

Have each small group prepare a frozen sculpture that best
communicates its theme or topic.
Students then share frozen images with the large group.

*Creating*

Using these sculptures as starting points, have each group begin
creating a scene.
Require elements that will challenge students to apply the
elements they have been learning about, such as:
  beginning, middle, end
  music
  poetry
  sculpture
  heightened moment
Use these same elements as criteria for evaluation.

## Days 7 & 8: Continue Small-Group Work on Theatre Piece

*Open Warm-up*

Design warm-ups to focus on specific skills that need to be
strengthened.

*Create and Rehearse Scenes*

Have students continue to work in their small groups.
Coach scenes and provide deadlines as the process demands.
To conclude the session, have each group preview a moment of
their piece for the class.

## Day 9: Small-Group Scene Performances

### Back Rubs and Line Work Warm-ups

Once they are standing in a circle, have students turn to their right and place their hands on that person's shoulders.
Coach a short back rub and breathing session to help everyone relax.
Next have everyone face the center of the circle and think of one line from his or her theatre piece.
One at a time, each person calls out a line and the ensemble repeats it back.
Coach for energy, volume, and emotion.
Have groups quickly rehearse their scenes, then come together for performance.

### Perform Scenes and Evaluate

Have groups perform their work.
Leave time at the end for feedback.
For evaluation, refer to the elements listed in Day 6.

### Reflection

Have students look for common threads running through all their scenes.
Or, they can identify moments they wish to expand upon.
Ideas and concepts for a more ambitious play production can develop from this kind of scene work.

## Images and Sculptures

Here students learn techniques of creating that do not depend on the spoken word. Thoughts and feeling are communicated through sculptures with the body. In my acting classes, this process has become a second language that can give life to a thought or feeling in a way words cannot. This process becomes an equalizer for those with diverse language skills or differing levels of verbal expression. Since much of this work is done in silence, it heightens focus and provides ample opportunities for physical expression.

## Day 1: A Language of Expression

### Directed Movement Warm-up

Have students walk, run, jog, freeze, or move in slow motion around the room.

Direct students to express different emotions with the body and face while moving.

Combinations of fast and slow energize and focus energy.

### Words and Images

Have students get into groups of six.

Ask them to select an emotion and identify at least five emotions contained within it.

For example, love can embody compassion, fear, power, jealousy, and humor.

Have groups create a sculpture for each of the five subemotions.

Finally, they are to connect the sculptures with transitions from one sculpture (and emotion) to the next.

Form a circle, dim the lights, add music, and have each group share its creation.

### Transforming Images

Remain in the circle.

Have a volunteer come to the middle of the circle and create a frozen body shape.

Ask a second volunteer to enter the circle, observe this frozen image, and transform it by creating another frozen image.

Once both players are frozen, ask others in the class to suggest stories of what might be happening in this frozen moment. Encourage several interpretations for each image.

Once several contrasting stories are shared, ask the first volunteer to unfreeze and bring in another volunteer to change the picture by adding a new frozen image.

Continue changing the images this way or have volunteers remain in the action so the image begins with two, but expands to include many volunteers.

### Reflection

Have students reflect on the notion of physical images as a language.

Encourage students to talk about whether they felt confused by or connected to the work.

Have them remember, share, and discus powerful moments.

## Day 2: Sculpting Each Other

### Sound and Movement Circle

Once students have come to the circle, have students create a sound and movement expression of how they feel using their entire body.

After each student shares, the entire group echoes back the sound and movement as a unified ensemble.

### Silent Sculpture Demonstration

Have students remain in the circle.

Ask two volunteers to come to the center.

Demonstrate the silent sculpting technique by having one student "sculpt" the other.

It is important that this is done entirely in silence and that communication is entirely physical.

A simple demonstration could be Person A sculpting Person B by first stretching her own hands toward the sky with a look of fear on her face.

As Person B assumes this position, Person A lets it go.

Person A can add further detail by physically demonstrating what she wants, or by gently moving the human sculpture into the desired position of expression.

### Silent Sculpting in Partners

Have everyone find a partner and practice sculpting each other until they become comfortable with the technique.

Maintain the silence.

Use soft music to heighten focus.

Once sculptures are complete, coach the sculptors to imagine a character or a story inspired by the image.

Encourage them to visit and watch each other's work.

### Sculpted Scenes

Groups of four, five, or six select one person to sculpt the others into a frozen dramatic moment.

The key here is for the person creating the sculpture not to preconceive an idea, but to allow the scene to emerge gradually while shaping the bodies.

### Sharing

Have students share their sculpted scenes and explain the stories embedded in their frozen moments.

End here, or use these story moments as starting points for more developed scene work.

## Day Three: Stories to Images

### Talking on Topics Warm-up

Have students walk randomly around the room.
Call out topics one at a time and ask students to talk spontaneously about that particular theme or issue.

### Faint by Numbers

Everyone counts off so that each person has a number.
The group walks around in a tight space.
When you call out a number, the person with that number "faints" and the entire group must catch that person as she or he starts to fall.
The group mills around again until the next number is called.
If the group is large, call out two numbers at a time.
Coach for concentration and trust through eye contact and silence.

### Story-telling in Groups

Have students get into groups of five and sit quietly in small circles.
Coach groups to sit with eyes closed, breathing together for a few minutes to focus and connect.
During this time begin to present a universal topic for story sharing, such as

I wish I had done it differently . . .
Once when I was treated unfairly . . .

Ask students to recall a story on the topic.
Keeping all eyes closed, have each person tell his or her story to the group.
The group's task is to listen and to visualize each story while the storyteller speaks.

### Imaging Stories

Have the groups decide on at least one story to present to the entire class.
Students build a sculpted image to communicate the essence of the story.

*Sharing*

All groups share their sculptures.
Once done, classmates ask one another what the images communicated.
Students can end by sharing the actual stories behind the sculptures with the class at large.

# Creating from Poetry

Poetry, literature, quotations, or any contemporary or historical writings are excellent sources for creating.

## IN ONE DAY: Silent and Spoken Poems

Below is a one-day activity containing two exercises based on poetry. First, the text of the poem is presented with images, sound and music, but not words. Second, the words of the poem are shared by the ensemble along with movement and action.

*Talk and Stop Warm-up*

Ask for six volunteers to stand in a line, shoulder to shoulder, facing the class.
The object of this exercise is for all six students to begin talking simultaneously on a suggested topic, and then on impulse, all stop talking at the exact same moment.
Begin by having someone suggest a topic.
Take turns so everyone has a chance.

*Poetry Jam in Small Groups*

Have students remain with their same group of six and sit in a tight circle.
Give to each group a few books of poetry.
Assign each group to look through the books and agree upon one poem with which to work.

*Create a Piece*

Assign students to create a piece that presents the entire text of the poem. However, they cannot use words—only images, sounds, pantomime, and music.
Coach students to create abstract images as well as realistic pantomime.

Have an ample selection of tapes from which students may choose.

### Each Group Performs

Have each group perform its piece.
Then, have the group run it a second time with someone outside the group reading the words of the poem as a narration.

### Reflection

Have the groups identify creative choices and make suggestions for improvement.
Encourage students to compare the effectiveness of the presentations with and without the use of words.
Often the pieces are more powerful without the words of the poem.

## IN ONE DAY: Ensemble Poetry

### Vocal Mirrors Warm-up

Everyone finds a partner and identifies Person A and Person B.
Assign a topic for Person A to talk about.
As Person A begins speaking, Person B attempts to talk along with Person A.
Then reverse and let Person B initiate the story.

### Circle Mirrors Warm-up

Have students move into groups of five and stand in a circle.
Each of the five takes a turn leading; the others mirror.
Change music with each leader.
After each person has led the group, have everyone remain in the circle, sit down, drop their heads, and relax.

### Small Groups Read Poem and Create

Hand out a preselected piece of poetry to each person.
Explain to the class that they will be staging this poem and assign each group a verse or section to work with.
Specify guidelines for creating, such as
    use movement
    use all lines in assigned text (spoken or sung)
    divide words and collage
    repeat words or phrases
    use instrumental music.

Each group reads the entire poem and then discusses how to stage its section.

Allow fifteen minutes for students to create a piece, reminding them to stay on their feet and keep the creating process active.

*Groups Share Their Work*

Each group performs its piece.

Allow time for critique.

Discuss how to expand on the work; for example, how to connect all the staged verses into one continuous piece.

I often refer to this process as collective reading, in that it can be applied to any text and serves as a motivation for reading as well as a process for creative expression. For example, if we are taking a field trip to see a play and the theatre sends us a study guide, I divide the class into small groups and give each group a section of the study guide to be read together and presented theatrically to the entire class. After bringing the material to life in this way, I assign the entire text as homework, which gets read because we have previewed it as a class.

# Universal Coachings

The following are coaching statements we find ourselves using in class, from the first day of the year to the last, with beginning and advanced students, at every stage of the creative process. When we first began to write the exercises down on paper, we found ourselves repeating these phrases in nearly every one. To avoid that kind of repetition we have listed these "universal" coachings here.

### Trust Your Impulses

Be spontaneous.
There is no right or wrong way to do an exercise.
Don't look for anybody's approval.
Stay out of your head.
Trust your body, your emotions, your intuitions.

### Believe in Yourself

Quiet your internal voices of doubt.
Don't compare yourself with others.
Don't ever say "I can't."

### Practice Respect

Respect yourself.
Respect others.
Respect the space you work in.
Learn from each other.
Strive not to demean anyone in the process.
Assume that everyone is doing their best.

### Commit

Commit to each exercise with your fullest energy.
You'll get as much out as you put in.
Leave attitudes and negative energy at the door.

### Take Risks

Go somewhere new.
Don't make the obvious choice.
Face a fear.
Reveal something unique.
Don't worry about looking silly.
Work with somebody you haven't worked with before.

### Relax

Take a deep breath.
Roll your shoulders.
If you're tense from your day, put those emotions into the work.
Don't worry about the outcome.

### Work with the Ensemble

Listen to each other.
Maintain eye contact.
Allow yourself to be affected by others.
Make connections.
Give and take focus.
Don't upstage others.
Share the stage.
Support each other's choices.

### Share Emotion

Be passionate about what you do.
Strive for depth.
Allow yourself to be vulnerable.
Reveal emotion in your face (or feet, or arms, or back).
Use objects to show how your character feels.
Let each movement be driven by emotion.

### Heighten the Action

Reveal more detail.
Show something new about your character.
Increase the stakes.
Intensify the conflict.

### Use All of Your Senses

Visualize your environment.
Imagine smells, tastes, and textures.
Listen to the music to create mood.
Listen to the music to heighten emotion.

### Stay Focused

Keep your concentration on your work.
Keep yourself from being distracted.
Close your eyes; drop your head.
If you feel like laughing, think of something serious.
Block out others who are breaking your concentration.

### Basic Rules for Improvisation

Don't begin a scene with a question.
Don't deny what the improv gives you.
Help your partner out.
Go along with what's happening.
Add new information to the scene.
Trust that the improv will develop.
Don't be yourself.

### Make Clear Character Choices

Go with your first instinct.
Know your objective.
What is your character thinking? Feeling? Wearing?
How old is your character?
How does your character move through space?
What gestures does your character make?
Share your character's voice.
What is the rhythm of your character's speech?

### Be an Engaged Audience

Watch attentively.
Focus all of your energy on the performer doing well.
Listen.
Offer comments to support the performer.

### Have Fun

Have fun.
Be playful.
Rediscover the child in yourself.

### Listen to Your Body

Notice where the tension is in your body. Let it go.
If your mind gets stuck, keep your body moving.
Listen to your body; it will give you more information.
Let your body lead you into the scene.
What emotion is your body communicating?
What character does your body suggest?
Take risks with your body.

### Vocalization

Project your voice.
Pronounce each word.
Vary the pace of your speech.
Open your mouth.
Sing your speech.
Pause.
Take a breath.
Lower/raise your pitch.

### Scene Work

Create a beginning, middle, and end for your scene.
Where does your scene take place?
Define the characters in your scene.
Choose a conflict for your scene.
Reveal your setting through the use of objects.
Freeze your scene in a heightened moment.
Create connections between your characters.
How you rehearse is how you perform.

# Organizing a Playwriting Festival

A student playwriting festival encourages individual students to share their stories through writing. Provided here is the outline used to organize a festival in Jan's class titled "Voices Have Power," in which selected work was produced, directed, and performed by students on stage. The process required about three months of work. In this process it is helpful to bring in artists or volunteers during the rehearsal process to observe and mentor students directing their peers. It is also helpful to limit the number of characters in each piece to about five, so student directors have a manageable number of peers to direct.

## Organizing the Festival

### Step 1: Freeing the Voice—Writing Activities

Begin with a variety of activities that inspire writing and instill confidence in students. Keep the festival inclusive and accessible by encouraging a variety of writing forms such as poetry, story, script, and journal entries. Provide tape recorders for those who prefer them to script spoken ideas.

### Step 2: Collecting and Sharing the Work

Have students read aloud excerpts of their own work or, each other's writings. Collect the work and provide feedback in written or conference form.

### Step 3: Selecting Work to Be Staged

Allow time for rewriting final drafts of the play scripts. Create a selection committee composed of students, teachers, community members, and guest artists. This committee will first generate the criteria for selecting plays, then read all entries anonymously and make final selections of plays to be staged.

### Step 4: Cold Readings

Schedule a series of cold readings of selected work. This is where scripts are handed to actors who read them aloud and informally, so that the playwright and the class can hear the words spoken.

### Step 5: Rewrites

A significant amount of time as well as assistance should be given to students as they rewrite their work. At this point in the process, it is helpful to involve skilled writers from outside of the class, working one on one with students.

### Step 6: The Production Process

During the rewriting process, student directors and stage managers are selected for each play. Each show is cast, either by audition, volunteers, or lottery. Job descriptions are written detailing each individual's responsibilities in the festival (see Job Description section following).

### Step 7: Rehearsal

During the rehearsal process, artists or volunteers are important as mentors for student directors, who hold fragile reins while directing their peers.

### Step 8: Performance

The performance style is best determined by the process and needs of the students involved. Entire plays can be performed or excerpts from several pieces can be collaged. Scenes can be presented as readings, with script in hand, or complete productions with costumes, sets, music, and lighting.

## Sample Job Descriptions

Provided here are the job descriptions created for the "Voices Have Power" Playwriting Festival put on by Jan's drama classes. Each play staged in the festival was assigned an artistic team including each of the following roles. Participants were responsible for reading, understanding, and practicing their job descriptions.

### Playwright

- Write the play.
- Produce a typed script.
- Accept and integrate criticism.
- Work with the artistic team.
- Complete rewrites by deadlines.
- Thoughtfully complete and submit reflection sheets (see sample).

### Student Director

- Work with mentor directors as assigned.
- Carry out the playwright's overall vision of the play.
- Direct blocking.
- Provide actor critiques.
- Run each rehearsal.
- Work cooperatively with the artistic team.
- Thoughtfully complete and submit reflection sheets.

### Actors

- Take direction.
- Memorize lines and blocking by deadline.
- Work at home on character development.
- Say focused, positive, and enthusiastic.
- Work with a changing script.
- Thoughtfully complete and submit reflection sheets.

### Stage Manager

- Support director in preparing show for production.
- Coordinate rehearsal space and weekly schedules.
- Take rehearsal attendance each day.
- Coordinate understudies as needed.
- Coordinate discussion between artistic staff members.
- Coordinate all technical aspects of the play.
- Run the show, starting with the technical rehearsals.
- Thoughtfully complete and submit reflection sheets.

### Technical Team

- Take direction from director and stage manager.
- Design lighting for the show.
- Design a musical score.
- Stay after school for several tech rehearsals.
- Run all lighting and music during the show.
- Thoughtfully complete and submit reflection sheets.

### Publicity and Promotion Team

- Write and produce festival program.
- Write and distribute press releases.
- Design, produce, and post flyers and posters.
- Design and execute a promotion plan.
- Design and produce tickets.
- Coordinate parent volunteers.

### Teacher

- Oversee entire project.
- Collect weekly reflection sheets and return with comments.
- Find, coordinate, and assign guest artists.
- Direct when necessary.
- Manage funds for festival.
- Provide learning and production resources.
- Run the house during performance.

## *Sample Weekly Reflection Sheet*

Your Name:

Date:

Title of the Play on Which You Are Working:

Your Role on the Artistic Team:

### WEEKLY REFLECTION SHEET

1. How did you spend your rehearsal time this week?

2. What problems did your artistic team encounter this week?

3. What solutions and discoveries did your artistic team develop this week?

4. What is your plan of action for next week?

# Press Release Sample

Below is an example of a press release written and distributed by the students in Jan's advanced acting classes. It includes

- a basic plot summary of the play
- the location and time of performances
- names of guest artists involved in the show's creation
- information about how the plays were created.

FOR IMMEDIATE RELEASE

CONTACT:     JAN MANDELL
             ST. PAUL CENTRAL HIGH SCHOOL
             ADDRESS
             PHONE NUMBER / FAX NUMBER

### PRESS RELEASE

Central Touring Theater, a multiracial group of students ages 15 to 18, will perform its final showing of the production *The Trial of Everyday Living*—an original play that demonstrates the courtroom drama of a society on trial. *Trial* brings to stage a creative and collective way of displaying the troubles and hardships a society allows to happen to its people. They will be closing their show on April 17th and 18th at Penumbra Theater in the Martin Luther King Center at 270 Kent Street. The night starts at 7:00 PM and the shows are preceded by a variety of local acts to create and promote community involvement.

Central Touring Theater has been creating and performing original work for over 17 years with the direction of Jan Mandell. They were joined this year by Yolande Bruce of Moore by Four, who assisted the cast musically and helped with choreography, and by local actor T. Mychael Rambo. The company has performed for over 10,000 people during their tour over the past three months. They have toured to the Minnesota Center for Arts Education, several high schools in the metropolitan area, and were recently awarded an honorarium at the Building Bridges Conference at Gustavus Adolphus College. The company is also a part of the Invisible Walls project and runs workshops for elementary, junior, and senior high school students as well as college students.

Have you ever wondered what would happen if a jury was forced to decide the innocence or guilt of a society on trial? How would you vote? Mr. Smith is chosen to represent his society in a court case that looks into the problems of education, self-esteem and image, responsibility, the effect of cycles of abuse, and other issues his society deals with. We encourage you to take the time to offer some media coverage to these talented and committed young community members who are using the arts to inspire positive social change. Additional information and publicity photos available upon request.

"[This show] is something that everyone in the community should experience. I was truly moved by the positive energy of these young people."

> Charlie Gray, Peace S.L.A.M.
> P.E.A.C.E. of St. Paul

# Research Methods

*The following information, written by Jennifer, outlines the research guidelines we developed for this project.*

In the first two years of our collaboration, I interviewed more than a hundred people associated with Jan's program: students, teachers, parents, administrators, alumni, college interns, college professors, community artists, and community theatre organizers. I also collected written assignments, letters, scripts, and articles generated by Jan's classes and the touring company.

I recorded each interview on tape and later transcribed each one onto the computer. Before each interview I explained who I was, the project that Jan and I were working on, and asked permission to use the interviewee's words and ideas in the construction of our book.

Because grant monies governed by Stanford University were used to fund our research, we used the Stanford University Human Subjects Guidelines to organize our research. We asked for formal release from each person interviewed.

For student interviewees under the age of eighteen, Jan signed a class release form as their teacher. Written and verbal information about our project was distributed to parents and school administrators. Interviewees over the age of eighteen signed their own release forms and were given written information about our process.

Stanford University Human Subjects Guidelines often stipulate anonymity to protect individual privacy. However, Jan's program and students had received wide media coverage for years prior to the beginning of our project, through newspapers, local and national television coverage, and national contests.

As a result, we did name Jan, Central Touring Theater, and her high school in this book. We named places and institutions affiliated with her work, such as the University of Minnesota and local theatre companies, if they were already known through publication and media coverage.

We used the full names of adults interviewed for the book if they were professional artists or educators who had already published their work in print or otherwise, such as guest artists in the classroom, professors, and Jan's principal.

We used first names of youth to identify quotations from their interviews. In documents such as journal entries and field note excerpts where the people described might not have been directly approached, all names were changed, combined, or left out. The same is true for references to others in interviews; for example, when parents discussed their children in interviews without the children present.

Students who kept journals for us were selected as likely to be responsible and enthusiastic about the project. I met with them personally to describe guidelines and writing techniques. They then kept journals in their own classes (where I was not present) over a period of months. They were compensated for their efforts with gift certificates to book or music stores.

When the story of a single individual receives sustained or focused coverage in the book, such as the stories about Levi in the Ensemble and rehearsal chapters, or the coverage of Colleen's dance concert in the performance chapter, we provided the text to the individual to read and respond to. For individual programs or institutions that receive extensive coverage, such as Jan's high school or my own 3-1-3 program, we asked the adult in charge to read the text and respond to it.

For stories referring to my own classes, I read the stories aloud to my students and asked permission to use their actual first names. If the students could no longer be located or are mentioned indirectly, I have changed their names.

# Annotated Bibliography

Included in this annotated bibliography are theatre and youth work titles we turn to the most frequently for ideas, exercises, and philosophical encouragement. Many of these volumes we keep right in our classrooms for long-range planning as well as last-minute emergencies. All of them can be applied easily to work with adolescents even if they are not written specifically for them.

Barranger, Milly S. 1995. *Theater: A Way of Seeing*. San Francisco: Wadsworth.

Now in its fourth edition, this textbook provides a comprehensive introduction to theatre arts. Rather than presenting a chronological history, Barranger examines how theatre offers new ways of seeing our world across boundaries of time, place, and tradition. Well-illustrated and indexed, this book reads both as a narrative of theatre and as a reference volume.

Boal, Augusto. 1992. *Games for Actors and Non-Actors*. London: Routledge.

Augusto Boal was first imprisoned and then exiled from his home country for the activist theatre work he did with farm laborers and the urban working poor under the dictatorship of the Brazilian government. This book contains hundreds of practical theatre games and exercises Boal used as he developed his Theatre of the Oppressed under the goal of using theatre for social change all over the world. Embedded in the exercises are Boal's beliefs that theatre is a form of knowledge and a vehicle for social change.

Boal, Augusto. 1995. *The Rainbow Desire: The Boal Method of Theatre and Therapy*. London: Routledge.

Boal's most recent book shows how his theatre methods can be used in a therapeutic context to enhance personal and group development. He describes his techniques in careful detail, so they can be easily adapted to educational and therapeutic situations with youth.

Bray, Errol. 1991. *Playbuilding: A Guide for Group Creation of Plays with Young People*. Portsmouth, NH: Heinemann.

Errol Bray has been creating original plays with youth in Australia for more than twenty years. His belief that all dramatic interactions with young people should result in performance elevates his work above a mere collection of exercises or games. Part philosophy, part how-to book, and part diary, this is a readable and complete introduction to original play construction. It also contains outlines of original plays created by youth as examples of what is possible.

Chapman, Gerald. 1991. *Teaching Young Playwrights*. Portsmouth, NH: Heinemann.

The founder of New York's Young Playwright's Festival, Gerald Chapman, writes a step-by-step approach to teaching young people the art of playwriting. Containing both philosophy and exercises, the book aims to eliminate the fears teachers and students have when faced with revealing themselves through dramatic writing. An introduction to role playing and improvisation techniques is offered as transition to setting pen to paper.

Chiefetz, Dan. 1971. *Theater in My Head*. New York: Little, Brown.

On thirteen consecutive Sundays in a church in Harlem, Chiefetz conducted a racially integrated theatre workshop in 1969. This book reads like a diary of his thoughts and observations as he watched the child participants come alive through drama. A practical program for stretching young people's perceptions of themselves and others is outlined, and is easily adapted to work with older youth.

Cleveland, William. 1992. *Art in Other Places: Artists at Work in America's Communities and Social Institutions*. Westport, CT: Praeger.

This book is a series of interviews by the author with artists who build and sustain communities through their art. Dramatic stories are retold by artists who work in "other places" such as hospitals, mental institutions, and community centers. Readers will find the projects described inspiring in the courage and originality they display.

George, Kathleen. 1994. *Playwriting: The First Workshop*. New York: Focal Press.

A day-by-day guide to running a playwriting workshop, this book is enjoyable and useful to read even if you do not intend to teach such a course. George weaves together traditional play construction theory and unique ideas for jump-starting creativity. The author illustrates her ideas with excerpts from well-known plays as well as from plays written by her students.

Gronbeck-Tedesco, John. 1992. *Acting Through Exercises*. Mountain View, CA: Mayfield Publishing.

The author of this college textbook set out to combine traditional and contemporary acting methods. The result is a collection of largely physical exercises illustrated with instructive photographs. The exercises are easily adapted for younger age groups. The introduction and appendices offer interesting insights into the author's research of acting methods.

Hagen, Uta, with Haskel Frankel. 1973. *Respect for Acting*. New York: Macmillan.

Uta Hagen made her Broadway debut in 1938 and has been acting professionally and teaching acting lessons ever since. This book outlines her philosophy of acting as well as offers exercises in categories such as Entrances, Basic Objects, Character History, and Talking to Yourself. Hagen uses examples from her own acting and teaching experiences to build her case that actors must show respect for their art.

Hamblin, Kay. 1978. *Mime: A Playbook of Silent Fantasy*. New York: Doubleday.

Though subject to stereotypes of white-faced actors trapped in invisible boxes, pantomime is an ancient performance art stressing physical discipline and nonverbal communication. This text follows the model of its subject—sparing in its use of the written word and generous in its use of photographs of people performing. Arranged from basic to advanced mime exercises, the book is so straightforward that it can be used successfully even by those with no background in pantomime.

Heathcote, Dorothy, and Gavin Bolton. 1995. *Drama for Learning*. Portsmouth, NH: Heinemann Educational Books.

Heathcote, Dorothy. 1976. *Drama as a Learning Medium*. Annapolis, MD: National Education Association.

British educator Dorothy Heathcote has argued vigorously for decades for drama as a method of learning. Especially interesting are her methods for turning a classroom into a historical setting for dramatic investigation. In these situations, Heathcote assigns herself a role within the extended improvisation that affords some leadership qualities while allowing her to play and learn with students.

Hodgson, John, ed. 1980. *The Uses of Drama: Acting as a Social and Educational Force*. New York: Methuen Books.

With this book, Hodgson offers a collection of essays by theatre scholars from Aristotle to the present. Included are issues such as drama as therapy, drama in education, and the search for creating new forms of drama.

Hodgson, John, and Ernest Richards. 1979. *Improvisation*. New York: Grove Press.

Written by two noted British theatre educators, this book examines how improvised drama helps people draw on their imaginative resources to extend their awareness of themselves and others. Philosophy is punctuated with practical activities and anecdotal material.

Johnstone, Keith. 1980. *IMPRO*. New York: Theater Arts Books.

Johnstone seeks to liberate the imagination, to cultivate the creative power of the child. Filled with activities, observations, and techniques, IMPRO demonstrates the methods the author has used in schools and colleges to encourage spontaneity and creativity through improvisational theatre games.

Lamb, Wendy, ed. 1992. *Ten Out of Ten*. New York: Bantam Books.

This is a collection of award-winning plays from the National Young Playwright's Festival. Written by authors under the age of eighteen, these plays deal with important issues in the lives of teenagers and offer usable material for school performances and classroom scene work. Included also are brief essays by the playwrights explaining how they conceived of and wrote their plays.

McCaslin, Nellie. 1996. *Creative Drama in the Classroom and Beyond*. Reading, MA: Addison-Wesley.

Now in its sixth edition, McCaslin's textbook is a well-known resource for college students and child educators. She discusses the theory behind using drama for the development of self-awareness, independent thinking, and cooperation in children. In addition, her texts offer practical activities in the use of drama in the classroom. Multicultural stories and poems are provided as resources for puppet making, improvisation, and original play production.

McGaw, Charles. 1980. *Acting Is Believing: A Basic Method*. New York: Holt, Rinehart and Winston.

Long used as an introductory textbook in college acting classes, McGaw's book is clearly organized into three parts: The Actor Alone, The Actor and the Play, and The Actor and the Production. In each section the author provides an explanation of method acting in plain language, well-explained nonverbal acting exercises, and more comprehensive scene work exercises. The author frequently uses scenes from well-known plays as the basis for exercises and includes three lesser-known short plays in the appendix for study and practice.

McLaughlin, Milbrey, Merita Irby, and Juliet Langman. 1994. *Urban Sanctuaries: Neighborhood Organizations in the Lives and Futures of Inner-City Youth*. San Francisco: Jossey-Bass.

This book examines successful youth-based community organizations in United States inner cities. While not all art-based, the organizations examined offer diverse examples of how to create, rehearse, and execute performances within community settings. Chapters focus on individual youth within the organizational settings.

Mda, Zakes. 1993. *When People Play People: Development Communication Through Theater*. New Jersey: Zed Books.

Mda is a South African poet, playwright, and professor of theatre who pioneered "protest theatre," a force that helped lead black South Africans to stand up to the apartheid government. This book offers his stories in diary form along with exercises that encourage everyday people to express themselves through theatre.

New Games Foundation. 1976. *The New Games Book: Play Hard, Play Fair, Nobody Hurt*. Ed. Andrew Fluegelman. San Francisco: The Headlands Press.

By now a well-known classic, this book is a collection of sixty creative games designed "not so much as a way to compare abilities, but to celebrate them." The "new" games collected and described in this volume encourage trust, cooperation, imagination, and healthy competition. Games are categorized as either moderate, active, or very active; can be played in groups small or large; and cost little, if anything, to execute.

Paley, Vivian. 1993. *The Boy Who Would Be a Helicopter*. Boston: Harvard University Press.

Written by a kindergarten teacher, this book may seem like an unlikely choice for working with adolescents, but Paley's ideas transfer across ages. In this examination of a single student who struggles to adapt to the school environment, the author details her method of having students tell her original stories, which they then translate into scripts and perform for the class at large. Also included is a thoughtful definition and rationale for inclusive classroom discipline.

Project Co-Arts. 1993. *Safe Havens: Portraits of Educational Effectiveness in Community Art Centers That Focus on Education in Economically Disadvantaged Communities.* Cambridge, MA: Harvard Project Zero.

Project Co-Arts. 1993. *The Co-Arts Assessment Handbook.* Cambridge, MA: Harvard Project Zero.

*Safe Havens* begins with the sentence, "In economically disadvantaged communities throughout the United States, in areas where outsiders may fear to tread and insiders tread with caution, safe havens exist." The safe havens of the book's title are inner-city community art centers, and the book examines six such exemplary groups in written portraitures, which include stories, interviews, and detailed observations. The *Assessment Handbook* is a more academic discussion of Project Co-Arts' unique method of assessing community art programs.

Schutzman, Mady, and Jan Cohen-Cruz, eds. 1994. *Playing Boal: Theater, Therapy, Activism.* New York: Routledge.

This collection of nearly twenty essays written by theatre practitioners from the Americas and Europe provides thorough accounts of the application of Boal's work to groups as diverse as a women's senior citizen group, a newspaper study group, and a group for street children in Brazil.

Spolin, Viola. 1963. *Improvisation for the Theater: A Handbook of Teaching and Directing Techniques.* Evanston, IL: Northwestern University Press.

Spolin, Viola. 1985. *Theater Games for Rehearsal: A Director's Handbook.* Evanston, IL: Northwestern University Press.

Spolin, Viola. 1986. *Improvisation for the Classroom.* Evanston, IL: Northwestern University Press.

Spolin's work is considered seminal in the development of improvisation for actors, directors, students, and teachers. Each book listed is filled with activities and strategies designed to get children and adults to use free play, imagination, and drama in a variety of settings. Each activity is geared toward age-specific participants and provides helpful comments for side coaching.

Stanislavski, Constantin. 1924. *An Actor's Handbook: An Alphabetical Arrangement of Concise Statements on Aspects of Acting.* Ed. and trans E.H. Hapgood. New York: Theatre Arts Books.

In the 1920s, Elizabeth Hapgood compiled and translated definitions of method acting terms from Stanislavski's major works. The result is this slim reference volume, which can be used as an introduction to Stanislavski and as a companion glossary when reading works that refer to method acting.

Stock, Gregory. 1985. *The Book of Questions*. New York: Workman Publishing.

This small book is simply a collection of 200 thought-provoking questions, some of which are hypothetical: "If you could spend one year in perfect happiness but afterward would remember nothing of the experience, would you do so?" and some of which are personal: "How do you react when people sing Happy Birthday to you in a restaurant?" The collection is an excellent source of conversation starters.

Unti, Gloria, and David Sarvis, with Gary Draper. 1990. *On Stage in the Classroom: Performance Art from K Through 8*. San Francisco: Performing Arts Workshop Book.

A practical classroom manual including model class plans, performance projects, and 150 classroom exercises for children. Focused on improvisation as a method of learning and creating, this book was compiled by the founder of the Performing Arts Workshop, an inner-city neighborhood arts program in San Francisco.

Way, Brian. 1972. *Development Through Drama*. New York: Humanities Press.

First published in 1966, this book still stands as one of the most important about drama as an educational tool. It does not contain specific exercises; instead, it is a manifesto of philosophy and observations about how all teachers can use drama in helping development of the young adult. Way also talks specifically about imagination, movement, sound, speaking, sensitivity, fighting, and violence and offers strategies for play making.